Recipes & REFLECTIONS

Anne-Marie
+
Année

Recipes & REFLECTIONS

A Journey of Food and Friendship
from The Inn at the Round Barn Farm
by Anne Marie DeFreest and Annie Reed Rhoades

First Edition
First Printing 1999
8,500

Copyright© 1999
A & A Enterprises
Rural Route 1, Box 247
East Warren Road
Waitsfield, Vermont 05673

Library of Congress Number: 98-075219
ISBN: 0-9665263-0-9

Photography
Front Cover: Paul Boisvert
Inside Jacket: Barrie Fisher
Back Cover: Paul Boisvert and Charlie Brown

Manufactured in the United States of America by
Favorite Recipes® Press
an imprint of

FRP

2451 Atrium Way
Nashville, Tennessee 37214

Project Leader: Charlene Sproles
Project Coordinator: Carolyn King
Art Director: Steve Newman
Book Design: Bill Kersey

Cooking from the Heart Catering at the Round Barn Farm designs and caters parties and
weddings throughout Vermont and New England. Annie Reed Rhoades also works as a private
chef for small groups and retreats. Anne Marie DeFreest is a consultant to the Bed and
Breakfast and Country Inn Industry. They can be reached at:
Cooking from the Heart Catering
The Inn at the Round Barn Farm©
Rural Route 1, Box 247
Waitsfield, Vermont 05673
Phone: 802-583-1091 or 802-496-2276
FAX: 802-496-8832
E-mail: roundbarn@madriver.com
www. innattheroundbarn.com

Additional copies of *Recipes & Reflections: A Journey of Food and Friendship*
from The Inn at the Round Barn Farm may be obtained by writing
to the above address or calling 800-721-8029.

For Jack and Doreen
With Gratitude and Great Appreciation
Annie and Anne Marie

Foreword

Storybook beginnings. Storybook endings. Life presents them every day—if only you take the time to find them. All you need is a thoughtful soul and a promising heart, and the poetry of fairy tales will manifest everywhere, even in your kitchen. And that's what this rather idyllic cookbook is all about.

As you browse through pages brimming with scones and streusels, swirls and salads, pastas and puddings, and so much more, you cannot help but dwell on the peeks behind the scenes. Sprinkled among the recipes are anecdotes, the consummate spices that give this cookbook a life of its own, a story. Recipe after recipe speaks to you, and you delight in the prospect of serving breakfast, dinner, and special-occasion foods that come highly recommended by Round Barn Farm guests, recipes that invite you to seek out their spirit as well as their taste.

An introspective tale of cooking along with the creation of one of America's most-talked-about bed-and-breakfasts is woven here with great craft. The result is a book that speaks volumes about what a cookbook ought to be—and that is a mirror of one's character and the everyday celebrations that have influenced it. Inside is a tasty epiphany of wondrous and easy culinary ideas. But Anne Marie also allows the reader passage to the ever-present charms that helped shape *Recipes & Reflections*—her family and her friends, especially Annie.

Annie and Anne Marie plan menus for the inn and their wedding business with the seemingly idealistic delight of two best friends at play. Each of their talents complements the other so that the end product in whatever they scheme together rings of genius hospitality and really clever, approachable cooking with a refreshingly gourmet touch.

Over the years, Annie—and later Anne Marie—talked with me about their desire to write a cookbook someday. Their voices never failed to resonate with commitment and enthusiasm as their pride in their work lit up their buoyant personalities.

The job of an innkeeper never stops, and the chore of pulling together a comprehensive collection of cherished kitchen recipes is a task most innkeepers never accomplish. With Annie as her cheerleading quarterback, innkeeper Anne Marie found a way to bring it all together for yet one more impression, for one more gift of herself to the traveler—this time for the armchair and the kitchen counter.

Those who have been fortunate enough to stay at The Inn at the Round Barn Farm will cozy up with this book as a reflection of their own discovery and journey to Vermont. The history of the inn is also the story of incredible friendships and relationships that—like the inn—began as something ordinary and developed into something unique and enduring. For those lucky enough to have this book, the inn's story of friendship and cooking will melt like a metaphor on the stovetop as the reader's personal past and present passions find their way into Anne Marie and Annie's culinary methods. You will ponder not only which recipe to choose to cook for something special, but also how to brew up your own memories and hopes for the future—as that "once upon a time" moment is now. Enjoy and get cooking.

Gail Greco

Author of Great Cooking with Country Inn Chefs,
The Romance of Country Inns and many other series.

Acknowledgements

Putting together a book of this size was no simple task, nor was it a singular task. I would like to thank David for bearing with me through the self-publishing book process. I know I did in five weeks what most publishers do in more than a year; without your support in caring for our children, it would not have been possible. Thank you Mom and Dad for loving me unconditionally and trusting my judgement as your business partner. And although you are both too young to read, thank you Elizabeth and David for being spirited children.

A.M.D.

I would like to thank the following people who directly or indirectly have provided inspiration for this book through their words of encouragement, sacrifice, support and belief in me: my parents, Lucy Modrak and John Skelly; my loving husband Don; my special son Ben; my beautiful stepdaughters Marah and Laurel; my stepfather Joe; my siblings John, Beth, Pattie, Chris, Rita, Joe Louis, Judy and Joe Jr., Geneva M., Maria S., Doug B. Thanks to Ann Freeman, Nanny and Breeze, Joyce and Nick N., Mary Laulis, Anuragi and Stephan Gersh, Jo Anna Jenkins, Jodi and Hadden, Kelly Wallace, Robert and Roselind, Jeff, Amy Mattinatt, Vern R., Sally Sweetland, Sara M., Paula A., L.M.P. and Alex, Ginny and John Roth, Andree and Stan. Thanks to my NECI support—Ellen McShane, Sandy Webb, Jim Miles, Lyndon Virkler and Spring Hill Family, especially Krisnabai, Lyra and Tinker.

A.R.R.

Together we thank the staff at The Inn at the Round Barn Farm, including Stephanie Koonz, Robert Badore, Kate Mahoney, Marnie DeFreest, Tracy Caslin, Tim O'Brien, Jennifer and Jack McDermott. Together we appreciate and thank the staff at CFH, especially Leslie Rossetto and Lisabeth Magoun. Thanks to our team, Phil Kiendl, Paul Hess, Kelly O'Hearn, Denise Fuoco, Kevin Dunn, Sue Shickler, Tom Raftery, Jim Gioia, Carol Charles, Michael Forest, Krista Shortle, Nancy Sargent, Chris Mayone, Erin Chase, Mili Chapel, Susanna McIlwaine, and Judi Gross.

We also would like to acknowledge the work and guidance of Patricia Floyd, Nancy Murray, Laurie Bartlett, Jackie Rose, Anthony Santor, Priscilla V. Special thanks to our photographer Paul O. Boisvert and to Barrie Fisher and Charlie Brown for their contributions as well. A very special thank you to Belinda Norris and the professional team at FRP. The last group of people we publicly acknowledge are our purveyors and "farmer friends" that include Wendy and Gene of Tunbridge Farms, David Hartshorn from Hartshorn Farm Stand, Willie Reed, Lisa Billiveau of Goose Creek Farms, Mason Wade of Roots Works, Allen at Squash Valley, Vince Gauthier at Valley Rent All, Jim Mahoney from Sysco, Tiffany Benzing, Very Small Donut Company, Laura Guion Calligraphy, John and Tim from North Country Linen and, last but not least, American Flatbread.

Anne Marie's Preface

Annie Reed Rhoades and I have been best friends since the day we met. Though polar opposites in business style, we are one and the same in dreams and aspirations. Throughout the years we have had many plans, one being to publish a cookbook together. Annie, the more experienced cook and ultimate collector of cookbooks, really wanted to create a book where the recipes worked and were all wonderful. My desire stemmed from a need to tell a story.

My journey as an innkeeper was not planned, nor was it intended to be traveled in a straight line. It started with a love . . . a love for life, a love for adventure, and a love for people who had soul.

My mother and father bought the old Joslin Farm located in Waitsfield, Vermont, in March of 1986. At the time, I was living in Boston and trying to find my way in broadcast journalism. The industry was flooded with new graduates and I found myself working more at my catering job at Harvard University than pursuing my journalism career. I was too young to see it at the time, but my communications degree was a universal asset. After a series of small setbacks, I ended up in Vermont halfway through my parents' project of opening a Bed and Breakfast.

The major restoration work had already painstakingly been completed when I had arrived in June of 1987. My mother was sorting furniture we had moved from our lifelong residence in New Jersey and scouting Vermont auctions for complementary pieces. The wallpaper was literally being hung around us as we planned each of the original seven guest rooms. My father retreated to the outdoors and had his hands filled with dirt and rocks, creating what is now known as one of Vermont's best landscaped inns. When I wasn't helping my mother make decorating decisions, I was at my corner desk at a typewriter trying to create a brochure and some sort of a reservations system.

Through the years we restored the landmark Joslyn Round Barn, added four guest rooms to the Inn, renovated some of the original guest rooms, and purchased the adjoining farm; the property boasts 235 precious acres. I have married, had two children, and have grown in a profession that has swept the nation.

Innkeeping is no longer a "hobby," but is a serious occupation. People are entering the field having done incredible research on properties, occupancy rates, and returns on investment. My family did not open our Bed and Breakfast with the same knowledge or studies. What we did bring with us was stamina, the ability to not only work hard but work smart, and a sense of humor. These qualifications are absolutely necessary in running a successful Bed and Breakfast or Country Inn.

My parents and I have spent the majority of our time at the Inn creating an atmosphere where people can feel safe. Christina Tree, author of Country Inn and Bed and Breakfast guidebooks, upon her first visit to our Inn perceived a very special "sense of place" that is felt the moment you enter. I believe that if people can feel secure in an environment, they have the chance to allow themselves to positively process their inner emotions and feelings. It is my goal as an innkeeper to provide the ultimate "sense of place" in regards to a facility or piece of property. It is my hope as an innkeeper that my guests leave The Inn at the Round Barn Farm with a more peaceful "sense of place" within themselves.

Annie and I have found our "sense of place." We believe being true to ourselves is the most important thing we can do for others. We self-published our cookbook because we wanted it to truly be our words, our food, and our story. I hope this is an inspiration to you to pursue what is in your heart. This cookbook/storybook is a gift from our hearts in hopes that it will touch yours.

Anne Marie DeFreest

Annie's Preface

"Like most other humans, I am hungry . . .
It seems to me that our three basic needs,
for food and security and love,
are so mixed and mingled and entwined
that we cannot straightly think of one without the other . . .
There is a communion of more than our bodies
when bread is broken and wine drunk."

MFK Fisher
Gastronomical Me

Cooking from the Heart was founded on the principle that people's hearts as well as their bodies are nourished when the staff who prepare the food use the highest-quality ingredients and care about the people they are cooking for.

My cooking career began fifteen years ago at Spring Hill in Ashby, Massachusetts, which offered "Opening the Heart Workshops." Originally trained as a therapist, I blindly accepted a job as a cook when there was no other position available. From that moment my entire relationship to people and food took on a whole new meaning. I learned that feeding people was much deeper than the physical ingestion of food, and that the people I was cooking for responded to the love and compassion I felt as I prepared their food. I learned the importance of making food look beautiful and became creative in combining flavors with fresh herbs since we served only vegetarian food. I learned to respect the quality and integrity of the ingredients we used and established a relationship with local farmers that resulted in my commitment to seek small farmers to grow my own food. I started a business called Cooking from the Heart and prepared and delivered food to more than forty-five families a week in the Boston area.

In 1988, I moved to Vermont and enrolled in the New England Culinary Institute a few years later in order to expand my knowledge since my prior training was a mix of intuition and trial by error, and luckily a passion for creating delicious food.

After graduation, Cooking from the Heart found its home at The Inn at the Round Barn Farm. There, my business relationship and close friendship with Anne Marie has continued to grow and blossom as we discovered the magic and synergy of combining our individual strengths and aspirations.

Today there is no doubt in my mind that the people we are feeding are experiencing and tasting something greater than the food itself. The joy and passion one feels for life is transcended from the provider to the recipient through the food. This is a philosophy I have always tried to impart to our staff and believe it is the secret to our success.

The recipes in this book are a starting point. It is my sincere hope that you, the reader, will take the recipes and make them your own. Present the food on a beautiful dish, garnish it with a fresh herb sprig or edible flower. Think about the people you are cooking for and become excited about what you are making and all the creative and fun ways to serve it. Begin to see food with new eyes. See the brilliant colors, shapes, and textures that nature has provided for us. Try to be in the present moment so that your attention is actually on what you are preparing. Most importantly, cook from your heart and allow yourself to be nourished by the joy of nourishing others.

Annie Reed Rhoades

Vermont Makes It Special

When one thinks of Vermont, the images of open fields and pastures filled with cows, integrity, and purity come to mind. Tourism is quickly replacing agriculture but it is still the big red barns, hand-picked stone-wall-lined fields, covered bridges, and tractors haying in the fields that tourists are coming to enjoy.

Based on that premise, Cooking from the Heart at The Inn at the Round Barn Farm is proud to be a member of the Vermont Fresh Network, an organization created by the Vermont Department of Agriculture that specifically promotes the relationship between farmer, grower, and chef.

During the months of June through October, we try to buy as much local organic produce as we can from our neighboring Vermont farmers. We have established a relationship with several growers who deliver their produce to us, fresh from their field to our door. Sometimes it means that we pay more than we would through our wholesaler, and people question how can we afford to pay so much for a tomato or head of lettuce. My response is always "How can we afford not to?"

The small farmers put their heart and soul into the food they grow, most of the time getting very little back on their return. But they continue to produce because they are committed to growing beautiful food that is pesticide free. We are committed to buying their product and helping make sure that they will still be around in ten years when vegetables in grocery stores are vacuum packed and irradiated.

The highlight of our work week is going to our local Farmers Market each Saturday morning and picking out fresh herbs and vegetables for our busiest catering day of the week. We are so proud of the food that we serve, knowing that not only are we cooking food with love, but that the ingredients were raised by people who care as much about the integrity of the raw product as we do about the final product. It is this collaborative effort that makes having a catering business in Vermont so special.

The Journey

Where is heaven? I say it's been found 14 miles south from Exit 10 off Interstate 89 in Vermont.

It's a drive most people are making for the first time, but at some point throughout the venture they realize it is an adventure that they will take over and over again.

The journey to The Inn at the Round Barn Farm is a gentle one. Vermont's most scenic highway Route 100 brings you through a valley still preserved by its farming and tourism-friendly businesses. The closest traffic light is 14 miles north in Waterbury. The nearest "Golden Arches" is 36 miles north in Stowe.

Historic Bridge Street in Waitsfield is the first landmark on your directions. The imagined quintessential Vermont town now becomes reality . . . a covered bridge, a country bakery, a specialty teddy bear shop where the animals secretly come to life after it's dark and all the humans have gone home. A popular spot where guests step back in time, surrounded by history and the sweet sounds of music, is vonTrapp Music and Design. No matter what season of the year it is, people visit the Christmas Tree Shop, where subtle holiday smells touch your senses . . . even in July.

Through the covered bridge and further up the way, the Inn seems to appear out of nowhere as you crest the hill on the East Warren Road. The sight of the Round Barn still takes even those familiar with the area by surprise. Changing with the seasons, this Vermont landmark is one graced with history and filled with friendly, warm hospitality. Welcome to our special place, an inn that is more than just a building. Welcome also to our incredible story.

It all began with two special people, the parents of five very diverse children—a licensed clinical social worker, a wholesale floral importer, an entrepreneur, a big-city private business investor, and me, an innkeeper. I have been fortunate enough to help determine the direction of this journey that only my parents could have started. This is not to say that my parents were the only ones capable of restoring this old farmhouse into an inn. They are, though, the only people who were capable of pursuing this particular vision, knowing when it was appropriate to let it pass from their hands into mine, and trusting enough to allow me to share it with my best friend Annie. That is why Annie and I have chosen to dedicate this collection of recipes and reflections to my mother and father, Doreen and Jack Simko.

The Pear

*The trademark and recognized symbol of Cooking
from the Heart Catering is the Seckel pear. Annie chose
this particular fruit because it resembles a heart
when turned upside down. The Seckel pear
is the aristocrat of all pears. Beautiful in appearance,
no two of the pears are exactly the same shape or color.*

*The pear and its progression throughout this cookbook
symbolizes the growth of a business and the evolution of this
cookbook. In Chapter One the pear is alone; in Chapter Two
it meets a friend; in Chapter Three another really cool
pear is added to the fruit bowl. By Chapter Eight,
the original pear is joined by many "friends"
and together they support one another.*

Annie and Anne Marie

Table of Contents

There's Nothing a Freshly Baked Cookie Can't Solve

*W*elcome to our Inn! *"The only requirement here is that you swap your winter snow boots for a pair of our comfortable house slippers."* We are always amused when returning guests sit down on the deacon's bench in the lobby and unpack their own slippers upon arrival.

It's not easy getting to our Inn. There's the getting out of work early to beat the traffic out of the city, there's the debate as to which is the fastest route here, and then there's that transformation that starts to happen in the car during the drive. Stress begins to ease from the mind, shoulders take a more relaxed position, and that sense of urgency that exists in everyday life begins to escape.

Our goal as innkeepers has been to create a place of beauty and peace, a refuge from the world. My mother and I have often said to each other . . . "You know, the world could blow-up and we would never know it!" The departure from a hectic world into a more peaceful place begins at The Inn at the Round Barn Farm with the smell of homemade cookies. We believe there's nothing that can't be solved by a freshly baked, rich, sweet treat.

A.M.D.

SWEET REWARDS

Round Barn Chocolate Chip Revolution Cookie

Margaret's Norwegian Raspberry Butter Cookies

Double Chocolate Oatmeal Cookies

Ginger Molasses Comfort Cookies

Almond Heart-Shaped Wedding Cookies

Strawberry Maple Almond Cookies

Lemon Ginger Shortbread Stars

ROUND BARN CHOCOLATE CHIP REVOLUTION COOKIE

1 1/2 cups flour
1 teaspoon cinnamon
1 teaspoon freshly grated nutmeg
1 teaspoon ginger
1 teaspoon cumin
1/2 teaspoon baking soda
1/2 teaspoon salt
1/8 teaspoon cayenne
Pinch of ground cloves
1 1/2 cups RainForest Crunch
    Sinful Snack Food
1 cup unsalted butter, softened
1 cup packed brown sugar
3/4 cup granulated sugar
1 teaspoon vanilla extract
2 eggs
3 cups old-fashioned or
    quick-cooking oats
1 cup chocolate chips

MAKES 4 DOZEN COOKIES

While on a lifelong mission to find the ultimate chocolate chip cookie, Kate Mahoney and I created this unusual "sinsation." There's just enough spice in this cookie to create some heat that invigorates the palate, making you want more and more of this crunch-filled combination.

A.M.D.

Sift the flour, cinnamon, nutmeg, ginger, cumin, baking soda, salt, cayenne and cloves together in a bowl. Combine 2 tablespoons of the flour mixture and the RainForest Crunch in a small bowl; set aside.

Beat the butter, brown sugar and granulated sugar in a large bowl until light and fluffy. Beat in the vanilla and eggs. Add the remaining flour mixture and stir until combined. Stir in the oats, chocolate chips and RainForest Crunch mixture. Drop the dough by teaspoons 2 inches apart on ungreased cookie sheets.

Bake at 375 degrees for 10 to 13 minutes or until golden brown. Cool on a wire rack.

NOTE: RainForest Crunch is a Brazil nut praline candy. If not available, substitute any nut-based praline candy. Should be broken into bite-size pieces.

MARGARET'S NORWEGIAN RASPBERRY BUTTER COOKIES

These cookies are dedicated to Amanda Gallant, an intern from the New England Culinary Institute, with whom I had the pleasure and privilege of working during the summer of 1996. This recipe was handed down from her grandmother, Margaret, who kept it a well-guarded secret. These are pure heaven. I told Amanda that I was sure in heaven everybody shared recipes and that Margaret would be overjoyed that so many people would be eating these amazing cookies. Amanda agreed, and here is the recipe for you to pass down to your family.

A.R.R.

1 cup butter, softened
1 cup confectioners' sugar
2 egg yolks, room temperature
1 teaspoon vanilla extract
2 cups flour
1 cup raspberry jam or preserves

MAKES 30 (2-INCH-SQUARE) COOKIES

Cream the butter and confectioners' sugar in a large bowl until light and fluffy. Beat in the egg yolks and vanilla. Add the flour and mix until combined. Reserve 1/3 of the dough and wrap in plastic wrap. Refrigerate until chilled.

Press the remaining dough on the bottom and partially up the sides of an ungreased 9x13-inch baking pan. Spread the raspberry jam over the dough. Roll out the chilled dough. Cut into 1/2-inch-wide strips. Place half the strips diagonally over the jam, arranging them all in 1 direction. Place the remaining strips diagonally in the opposite direction, forming a crisscross diamond pattern.

Bake at 350 degrees for 25 minutes or until light golden brown. Cool before cutting into squares. Cut into 2-inch squares.

DOUBLE CHOCOLATE OATMEAL COOKIES

I love to forget to add the oats in this cookie. Forgetting them makes for an overly rich chocolate cookie that melts in your mouth. I also substitute white chocolate chips for the milk chocolate chips, which gives them a totally different taste sensation.

A.M.D.

1¼ cups flour
½ cup baking cocoa
1 teaspoon baking soda
½ teaspoon salt
1 cup butter or margarine, softened
1 cup packed brown sugar
½ cup granulated sugar
1 teaspoon vanilla extract
2 eggs
1 (11-ounce) package (2 cups) milk chocolate chips
1¾ cups quick-cooking or old-fashioned oats

MAKES 4½ DOZEN COOKIES

Combine the flour, cocoa, baking soda and salt in a small bowl. Cream the butter, brown sugar, granulated sugar and vanilla in a large mixer bowl until light and fluffy. Add the eggs 1 at a time, beating well after each addition. Gradually beat in the cocoa mixture. Stir in the chocolate chips and oats. Drop the dough by rounded tablespoons 2 inches apart on ungreased cookie sheets.

Bake at 375 degrees for 10 to 12 minutes or until the edges are set. Let stand for 2 minutes before removing to a wire rack to cool completely.

"Never eat more than you can lift."
—Miss Piggy

GINGER MOLASSES COMFORT COOKIES

This recipe comes from Laurie Roth Bartlett, who owns Alta Day Spa in town and does many of our brides' hair and make-up. Laurie is also an amazing chef and is always making us delicious treats. These cookies make you feel better and would comfort anyone who needed a little tender loving care.

A.R.R.

4¹/2 cups flour
4 teaspoons baking soda
4 teaspoons ginger
2 teaspoons cinnamon
1 teaspoon ground cloves
¹/2 teaspoon salt
1¹/2 cups butter, softened
2 cups packed brown sugar
2 eggs, room temperature
¹/2 cup molasses
Granulated sugar

MAKES ABOUT 50 COOKIES

Combine the flour, baking soda, ginger, cinnamon, cloves and salt in a bowl. Cream the butter and brown sugar in a large bowl until light and fluffy. Add the eggs 1 at a time, beating well after each addition. Beat in the molasses. Stir in the flour mixture. Chill the dough for 15 minutes. Drop the dough by rounded tablespoons, or use a 1-ounce scooper, into a bowl of granulated sugar, coating only 1 side. Place dough rounds, sugar sides up, 2 inches apart on greased cookie sheets (the cookies spread out as they bake).

Bake at 375 degrees for 10 to 15 minutes or until set but still soft in the middle. Cool on a wire rack.

Almond Heart-Shaped
Wedding Cookies

Almond Heart-Shaped Wedding Cookies

1 cup sugar
6 ounces almonds, lightly toasted
   and coarsely chopped
3/4 cup unsalted butter, cut into
   12 pieces
1 teaspoon almond extract
1 egg, room temperature
2 cups flour
1/4 teaspoon salt
Flour for dipping

**Makes 3 dozen (2-inch)
hearts**

At Round Barn wedding receptions we place a beautifully garnished glass platter filled with these cookies and chocolate-dipped strawberries on each dinner table after the main entrée is served but before the cake is cut.

A.M.D.

Process the sugar and half the almonds in a food processor, pulsing until blended. Add the butter pieces and almond extract. Process for 45 seconds. Add the egg. Process for 60 seconds. Combine the 2 cups flour and salt in a bowl. Add to the food processor. Process until most of the flour has been incorporated. Add the remaining almonds. Process until the dough is combined and starts to come together. Turn the dough onto a lightly floured surface and divide in half. Shape each half into a ball and flatten slightly to form a round disk. Wrap the disks in plastic wrap. Refrigerate until chilled.

Remove the dough from the refrigerator to soften slightly before rolling. Place each disk of dough between 2 pieces of parchment paper, waxed paper or plastic wrap. Roll out 1/4 inch thick. (Roll evenly, always beginning at the center. Roll the pin outward each time in a different direction. Lift the rolling pin after each roll. Do not roll the pin back and forth.)

Peel off the top sheet of paper. Dip a 2-inch heart-shaped cookie cutter into flour and use to cut out the cookies. Cut out the hearts as close together as possible to avoid rerolling the dough. Use a metal spatula to transfer the cut-out cookies to ungreased cookie sheets.

Bake at 350 degrees for 10 to 12 minutes or until the edges are golden brown, rotating the cookie sheets halfway through the baking time. Cool on a wire rack. Store in an airtight container for up to 1 week if they last that long!

STRAWBERRY MAPLE ALMOND COOKIES

This recipe and words of wisdom below were given to me by my friend, Amy Mattinat, on my 40th birthday when I asked my friends to bring their favorite recipe instead of gifts. Amy wrote, "I've made these cookies a million times...and I still love to make them and eat them." I totally agree—they are quick to make and the recipe is so simple that you can make them from memory after a few times.

A.R.R.

3 cups almonds

3 cups rolled oats

3 cups flour

1/2 teaspoon cinnamon

Pinch of salt

1 1/2 cups vegetable oil

1 1/2 cups Vermont maple syrup

1 cup strawberry preserves or jam

MAKES 5 DOZEN (2-INCH) COOKIES

Process the almonds and oats in a food processor until pulverized. Pour into a large bowl. Stir in the flour, cinnamon and salt.

Whisk the oil and maple syrup in a bowl until well blended. Add to the almond mixture and stir until combined. Chill for 10 minutes.

Roll the dough by 2 tablespoons or 1-ounce scoops into balls. Place 2 inches apart on greased cookie sheets. Make an indentation in the center of each ball with your thumb. Fill with the strawberry preserves, being careful not to overfill.

Bake at 350 degrees for 15 to 20 minutes or until golden brown. Cool on a wire rack.

ALOHA VERSION: Substitute 3 cups macadamia nuts for the almonds. Add 1/2 cup chopped toasted almonds with the flour. Substitute guava or apricot jam for the strawberry preserves.

LIGHTER VERSION: Substitute 3/4 cup unsweetened applesauce for 3/4 cup of the oil.

"Now is the closest approximation of eternity that this world offers. It is the reality of 'now' without past or future, that the beginning of the appreciation of eternity lies. For only 'now' is here."

LEMON GINGER SHORTBREAD STARS

2¹/3 cups flour

³/4 cup confectioners' sugar

2¹/2 teaspoons ground ginger

¹/2 teaspoon salt

1 cup butter, softened

2 teaspoons grated lemon zest

¹/2 teaspoon vanilla extract

¹/2 teaspoon lemon extract

¹/2 cup chopped crystallized ginger

MAKES 3 DOZEN SMALL COOKIES

The first time I ate these cookies I knew I had to get the recipe from my friend Jean, who found them in a cooking magazine. They have become a regular on our menu ever since.

A.R.R.

Combine the flour, confectioners' sugar, ground ginger and salt in a mixing bowl. Beat the butter in a large bowl until light and fluffy. Add the lemon zest, vanilla and lemon extract. Beat in the crystallized ginger. Stir the flour mixture, 1 cup at a time, into the butter mixture until blended.

Divide the dough in half and shape into 2 balls. Wrap the balls in plastic wrap. Refrigerate until chilled. Roll the chilled dough out to a ¹/3-inch thickness. Cut with cookie cutters such as star or heart shapes. Place the stars 1 inch apart on greased cookie sheets.

Bake at 325 degrees for 24 minutes or until golden brown around the edges. Cool the cookies on the cookie sheets.

VARIATION: Instead of shaping the dough into balls, divide into 2 equal portions and roll each portion into a log. Wrap the logs in plastic wrap. Refrigerate until chilled. Cut the chilled logs crosswise into ¹/3-inch slices. For variety, drizzle cookies with melted chocolate.

Special Friends &
Time to Unwind with
Afternoon Hors d'Oeuvres

*A*fternoon hors d'oeuvres at the Inn have evolved over the years. When we first opened in the fall of 1987, my father Jack would produce something tasty and unusual out of the Inn's refrigerator about ten minutes before our afternoon guests were due to arrive. It soon became obvious that Jack was able to create incredible hors d'oeuvres out of miscellaneous refrigerator ingredients. Just like most of my mom's cooking, it was best enjoyed in the moment, because we never saw the same dish twice. Jack's creations were spontaneous and scrumptious.

With the arrival of spring, Jack fled the kitchen to the outdoors, leaving behind his task of preparing the afternoon goodies. My mother and I assumed that responsibility, often flipping a coin to see who would end up in the kitchen. Luckily a few great cookbooks guided our way and everyone was pleased.

After a few years of running the Inn successfully, we were able to hire staff. Each and every one of these very special people added a new dimension and element to the afternoon hors d'oeuvres period. Allison, with her irreplaceable smile and sense of humor, would whip something up in a jiffy, but it was really her personality and joy for life and our guests that made the afternoon special. Jane had some formal culinary background, and often surprised us with her innovations. We never knew *what to expect with Jane, but we could always count on great taste, elegant presentation, and grace. Annie brought to the afternoon hors d'oeuvres time a new creativity and flair.*

Annie Reed Rhoades and I met at an innkeepers' dinner. She was working as resident innkeeper at the Mad River Inn, owned by her sister and brother-in-law. A few days after our first meeting, I swept her out of the Valley for an afternoon of fun in Burlington and later learned she had not been out of the Valley in six months! Thus began our incredible friendship.

Soon Annie came to work at The Inn at the Round Barn Farm as an assistant innkeeper. My mom and I would go off to accomplish ten hours of errands in about six, and we would come back to great smells, soothing music, and unbelievable afternoon hors d'oeuvres. With what seemed like little or no effort, Annie would single-handedly run the Inn, and take care of our guests as if they were all her closest friends. The following recipes are from those who have helped create the special environment at The Inn at the Round Barn Farm. Many of the recipes belong to Annie Reed Rhoades. Over the years our preparation of food has become more sophisticated and more stylish.

The season in which you choose to visit The Inn at the Round Barn Farm will determine what you will taste. Because we have a commitment to use only the freshest ingredients, and to prepare seasonal menus, you may enjoy a sinful baked Brie with berries in the hot months of summer or enjoy a similar version with red onion compote and cranberry chutney, pears, and spiced apples in the fall. Where you'll enjoy your hors d'oeuvres is also determined by the season. In the summer months we find our guests scattered among the Holstein-painted Adirondack chairs along the back 40. In the cooler months, guests stick closer to the roaring fire in the book-lined library, sipping sherry and relaxing with a book. No matter what the location, the purpose is similar. This is the time that all of our guests start to unwind. Tensions that were carried along with the journey slip away with the involvement of interesting conversations with strangers, soon to be friends.

A.M.D.

SAVORY AFTERNOON
HORS D'OEUVRES

Savory Artichoke Cheesecake Spread

Hot Shrimp and Crab Dip

Shrimp Salsa with Fresh Horseradish

Sun-Dried Tomato and Basil Pesto Torta

Smoked Salmon Pinwheels with Cucumber Salsa

Goat Cheese and Summer Chutney on Garlic Crostini

SAVORY ARTICHOKE CHEESECAKE

CRUST:

2 teaspoons butter, softened
¼ cup fine dry bread crumbs
¼ cup grated Parmesan cheese
*1 tablespoon finely chopped fresh
    Italian herbs*

CHEESECAKE

16 ounces cream cheese, softened
1 cup crumbled feta cheese
1 cup sour cream
3 eggs
1 (14-ounce) can artichoke hearts
1 small red bell pepper
1 small green bell pepper, chopped
*6 green onions, white bulbs and
    ½ inch of green tops, chopped*
1 large clove of garlic, crushed
1 tablespoon chopped fresh tarragon
1 tablespoon chopped fresh basil
1 teaspoon salt
½ teaspoon pepper

GARNISH

Reserved artichoke hearts
Reserved red bell pepper strips
6 fresh basil leaves
¼ cup chopped parsley

SERVES 20

This is a delicious spread with a savory taste. It is a great make-ahead hors d'oeuvre to serve at home or take to a party.

A.R.R.

CRUST: Grease a 9-inch springform pan with the butter. Combine the bread crumbs, Parmesan cheese and herbs in a bowl. Add to the buttered pan, rotating and tilting the pan to coat the bottom and side with the crumb mixture. Tap out any excess crumb mixture from the pan and reserve.

CHEESECAKE: Process the cream cheese in a food processor until fluffy, scraping the sides of the container. Add the feta cheese and sour cream. Process until smooth. Add the eggs, beating until smooth.

Reserve 2 of the artichoke hearts for garnish. Drain and chop the remaining artichoke hearts and add to the cheese mixture. Cut 4 small strips from the red pepper; reserve for garnish. Chop the remaining red pepper and add to the cheese mixture with the green pepper, green onions, garlic, tarragon, chopped basil, salt and pepper. Pulse until thoroughly blended. Spoon the cheese mixture into the prepared springform pan.

Bake at 350 degrees for 55 minutes or until golden brown. Cool to room temperature. Refrigerate, covered, in the pan for at least 2 hours. Remove from the pan. Pat the reserved crumb mixture on the outside edge of the cheesecake.

GARNISH: Arrange the reserved artichoke hearts, reserved red pepper strips, basil leaves and parsley decoratively on top of the cheesecake. Serve with toast points or crackers.

NOTE: One teaspoon of dried tarragon and 1 teaspoon of dried basil can be substituted if fresh herbs are not available. Also, a thin layer of sour cream can be spread on top if desired.

HOT SHRIMP AND CRAB DIP

8 ounces cream cheese, softened
2 tablespoons chopped onion
1 tablespoon milk
3 ounces cooked crab meat, flaked
3 ounces cooked shrimp, coarsely
    chopped
1/2 teaspoon minced garlic
1/2 teaspoon horseradish
Salt and pepper to taste
Slivered almonds

SERVES 12

Combine the cream cheese, onion and milk in a medium bowl, mixing until slightly blended. Add the crab meat, shrimp, garlic, horseradish, salt and pepper. Stir until well blended. Spread the mixture evenly in a shallow 1-quart baking dish or 9-inch pie plate sprayed with nonstick cooking spray. Sprinkle the almonds over the top. Bake at 350 degrees for 15 to 20 minutes or until heated through. Serve hot with an assortment of crackers or herb toasts.

SHRIMP SALSA WITH FRESH HORSERADISH

This is a recipe that I created one day with leftovers from the refrigerator for a gathering at Charlie Brown and my sister Rita's house. It was a big hit and we now serve it all the time at parties and events.

A.R.R.

1 pound ripe tomatoes
1/4 cup chopped onion
1/4 cup chopped green bell pepper
1/2 jalapeño pepper, seeds removed
2 sprigs fresh cilantro
1 cup chili cocktail sauce
1/4 cup freshly grated horseradish
6 large cooked shrimp, diced
1 green onion, finely chopped

MAKES ABOUT 5 CUPS

Pulse the tomatoes, onion, green pepper, jalapeño pepper and cilantro in a food processor just until combined. Pour into a large serving bowl. Stir in the chili cocktail sauce, horseradish, shrimp and green onion. Season to taste with additional horseradish. Serve with black bean or blue corn tortilla chips.

NOTE: If fresh tomatoes are not available, substitute one 28-ounce can organic whole peeled tomatoes, drained and chopped. May also substitute prepared horseradish for fresh horseradish.

Sun-Dried Tomato and Basil Pesto Torta

This recipe was adapted from Michele Braden's "Fast & Fabulous Hors d'oeuvre" book. It is one of our favorite and most requested recipes. We make it in heart shapes for weddings and in tree shapes for winter holiday events.

A.R.R.

Cheese Filling

8 ounces cream cheese, softened

4 ounces (1/2 cup) feta cheese

1/2 cup unsalted butter, softened

1 medium shallot, chopped

1 clove of garlic, chopped

2 teaspoons dry sherry

1/2 teaspoon salt

Sun-Dried Tomato Pesto

1 cup oil-packed sun-dried
    tomatoes, or 1 cup rehydrated
    dry-packed sun-dried tomatoes
    plus 1/4 cup olive oil

1/4 cup tomato paste

Olive oil

1/2 cup grated Parmesan or pecorino
    Romano cheese

Cheese Filling: Process the cream cheese, feta cheese, butter, shallot, garlic, sherry and salt in a food processor until smooth. Remove from the food processor to a bowl; set aside. Wash out the food processor work bowl.

Sun-Dried Tomato Pesto: Process the sun-dried tomatoes and tomato paste in a food processor until smooth. (If using the rehydrated sun-dried tomatoes, add the 1/4 cup olive oil with the tomatoes.) Add enough olive oil to make a spreadable pesto consistency. Add the Parmesan cheese. Pulse until combined; set aside. Wash out the food processor work bowl. Makes 1 1/2 cups.

SPINACH BASIL PESTO

¹/₃ cup olive oil

2 cloves of garlic

2 cups fresh spinach leaves,
  stems removed

²/₃ cup fresh basil leaves,
  stems removed

¹/₂ cup grated Parmesan or pecorino
  Romano cheese

ASSEMBLY

1 cup pine nuts

Fresh basil sprigs (optional)

SERVES 12 TO 15

SPINACH BASIL PESTO: Process the oil and garlic until the garlic is minced. Add the spinach and basil. Process until smooth. Add the Parmesan cheese. Pulse until combined; set aside. (The spinach in this pesto keeps it bright green, unlike basil pesto that can quickly turn brown. If it is not used within 2 days, it should be frozen as it has a very short shelf life.) Makes ³/₄ cup.

ASSEMBLY: Line a 3-cup mold with plastic wrap, allowing at least 2 inches to hang over the sides of the mold. Sprinkle ¹/₃ of the pine nuts over the bottom of the mold. (We usually make a design with the pine nuts so that when you turn it over to unmold, the design is on the top.) Next, layer half the sun-dried tomato pesto, half the cheese mixture, all the spinach basil pesto, ¹/₃ of the remaining pine nuts, the remaining cheese mixture, remaining sun-dried tomato pesto and remaining pine nuts. Cover the mold with plastic wrap, pressing lightly so that all the edges are covered. Refrigerate for at least 3 hours. Uncover the mold and invert onto a serving platter. Carefully peel off the plastic wrap. Garnish the torta with fresh basil sprigs. Serve with star- or heart-shaped toasts or crostini.

NOTE: Once the cheese filling is made, it needs to be used in assembling the torta. It cannot be made in advance separately and refrigerated or it will become too firm to spread in the mold. This recipe can be doubled or tripled.

BASIL PESTO VARIATION: Process ¹/₄ cup peeled cloves of garlic in a food processor until chopped. Add 6 cups packed fresh basil leaves, stems removed. Pulse until chopped. Add ¹/₂ cup grated Romano cheese. Pulse until blended. With the food processor running, drizzle in 1 cup olive oil. Process until thoroughly combined. Basil pesto may be used in place of the spinach basil pesto. Use 1 cup of the basil pesto in the torta. Makes 2 cups.

Smoked Salmon Pinwheels with Cucumber Salsa

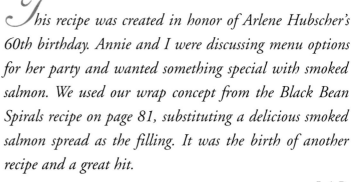

This recipe was created in honor of Arlene Hubscher's 60th birthday. Annie and I were discussing menu options for her party and wanted something special with smoked salmon. We used our wrap concept from the Black Bean Spirals recipe on page 81, substituting a delicious smoked salmon spread as the filling. It was the birth of another recipe and a great hit.

L.A.R.

Salmon Filling

16 ounces cream cheese, softened
$1/4$ cup chopped red onion
1 ounce smoked salmon
$1^1/_2$ tablespoons lemon juice
1 tablespoon drained capers
2 sprigs fresh dill, stems removed

Cucumber Salsa

1 cup peeled, seeded and minced cucumber
2 tablespoons minced red onion
2 tablespoons minced red bell pepper
2 tablespoons minced yellow bell pepper
2 tablespoons chopped fresh dill
$1/4$ cup rice wine vinegar
$1/4$ cup sugar

Assembly

6 (8-inch) flour tortillas

Makes about 72 pinwheels and $1^1/2$ cups dip

Salmon Filling: Process the cream cheese, red onion, salmon, lemon juice, capers and dill in a food processor until smooth. Transfer to a bowl. Refrigerate, covered, for 1 hour.

Cucumber Salsa: Combine the cucumber, red onion, red pepper, yellow pepper and dill in a bowl. Bring the vinegar and sugar to a boil and cook until clear. Cool completely. Add the vinegar mixture to the cucumber mixture. Refrigerate, covered, until ready to use. Drain before using.

Assembly: Lay the tortillas out in a row. Spread $1/3$ cup salmon filling evenly over the bottom $3/4$ of each tortilla. Starting at the bottom, tightly roll up each tortilla. Wrap each tightly in plastic wrap. Refrigerate for 2 hours or until firm.

Unwrap the tortillas. Slice both ends off of each tortilla and discard. Then slice each crosswise at $1/2$-inch intervals to form pinwheels. Arrange the pinwheels in a concentric pattern on a serving platter. Place 1 teaspoon cucumber salsa on 1 side of each pinwheel.

Note: The leftover salmon filling makes a delicious dip. Refrigerate, covered, for up to 1 week.

GOAT CHEESE AND SUMMER CHUTNEY ON GARLIC CROSTINI

This recipe was inspired by Tim Benzing, a talented chef who prepared the food for my culinary school graduation party. This was served on the side of a baby green salad. At the Inn, we serve it as an hors d'oeuvre. It takes minutes to make if you have chutney on hand, and the flavors are incredible!

A.R.R.

SUMMER CHUTNEY

4 cups (1 pound) chopped ripe peaches

2 medium onions, coarsely chopped

1 small red bell pepper, seeded and chopped

1 cup golden raisins

2 small hot red peppers, seeded and minced

$^1/_4$ cup grated gingerroot

$^1/_4$ cup minced crystallized ginger

$2^1/_2$ cups packed brown sugar

2 cups white vinegar

Pinch of cloves

1 teaspoon salt

1 teaspoon cinnamon

MAKES 3 CUPS CHUTNEY

ASSEMBLY

4 ounces goat cheese

Garlic Crostini

MAKES 8 TO 12 CROSTINI

SUMMER CHUTNEY: Combine the peaches, onions, red bell pepper, raisins, hot red peppers, gingerroot, crystallized ginger, brown sugar, vinegar, cloves, salt and cinnamon in a large stainless steel saucepan. Bring to a boil; reduce the heat. Simmer for $1^1/_2$ hours or until the liquid has been absorbed and the chutney has thickened. Cool to room temperature before using.

GARLIC CROSTINI: Slice narrow French bread into $^1/_4$-inch rounds. Brush with olive oil or clarified butter (page 93). Sprinkle with chopped garlic. Bake at 350 degrees for 5 minutes or until golden brown.

ASSEMBLY: Spread $^1/_2$ to $^1/_3$ ounce goat cheese over each garlic crostini. Spoon 2 teaspoons chutney over the goat cheese, spreading evenly. Serve on a platter. Garnish with fresh herbs.

NOTE: The leftover summer chutney can be stored, covered, in the refrigerator for up to 2 weeks.

Friday Night Winter Dinners

hen we opened the Inn we established three specific areas of business that would not become our specialties: selling all-inclusive packages, marketing to families and groups, and serving dinner. Because innkeepers never stop, and because discipline is the key to longevity in this business, my mother, father, and I chose instead to limit our services to a Bed and Breakfast and not a full-service Country Inn. We defined a very specific market and were successful in not deviating from it for many years. However, our guests often asked for dinner service, especially in the cold winter months. Chef Leslie Rossetto prepared and served the first Friday Night Dinner at the Inn on December 5, 1997. It is a fact that Leslie Rossetto is the most talented "self-taught" chef I have ever met.

Friday Night Dinner at the Inn brought a whole new experience to our guests. Once we got adjusted, dinner service ran smoothly. I resisted because I wanted nothing to do with anything that was going to extend the Innkeeper's hours on Friday nights. In fact, the opposite proved true. On the last Friday night dinner of the winter, every guest was safe and sound, well fed, and settled for the evening by 8:30 p.m.! This is unheard of with Friday night winter arrivals that consist of weekend warriors. I felt at peace knowing that all of our guests had arrived safely, started their weekend with an incredible meal, and did not have to go back out to dangerous snow-covered roads to find a meal after hours of driving. Instead, they were going out for moonlit walks through freshly fallen snow.

Annie and I dedicate this chapter to Leslie Rossetto. Her love for her Italian heritage is apparent in all she does. The teachings of her parents and grandparents have served her well. She is a gifted chef, an amazing people person who is willing to share her knowledge of cooking and fine wines freely. As devoted friend and partner, she is the third pear in the bowl.

A.M.D.

Friday Night Winter Dinners

Homemade Ravioli with Fresh Ricotta,
Mozzarella and Grilled Radicchio

Roasted Tomato Fennel Sauce

Tri-Colored Salad with Aged Balsamic Vinegar,
Olive Oil and Shaved Parmesan Cheese

Pork Chops Delores

Aldo's Garlic Carrots

Arugula Mashed Potatoes

Portobello Wellington with Boursin Cheese

Leslie's Key Lime Pie with Vermont Maple Syrup
and Whipped Cream

RAVIOLI WITH GRILLED RADICCHIO

This fabulous ravioli is best served piping hot with our Roasted Tomato Fennel Sauce.

L.A.R.

PASTA DOUGH

3/4 cup (4 ounces) all-purpose flour
2/3 cup (4 ounces) semolina flour
2 eggs
1 egg yolk
1 tablespoon olive oil
1 1/2 teaspoons salt
2 tablespoons all-purpose flour

RAVIOLI FILLING

1 head radicchio, cut into quarters
2 tablespoons olive oil
1 cup fresh ricotta cheese
1 cup diced fresh mozzarella cheese
1 egg
1 tablespoon chopped shallot
1 tablespoon chopped garlic
1 teaspoon salt
1 teaspoon fresh cracked pepper
1 teaspoon chopped fresh parsley
1 teaspoon chopped lemon thyme

ASSEMBLY

36 small flat-leaf parsley leaves
1 egg
1 tablespoon water
Roasted Tomato Fennel Sauce
    (page 39)

MAKES 12 (4-INCH) RAVIOLI

PASTA DOUGH: Process the 3/4 cup all-purpose flour, semolina flour, eggs, egg yolk, oil and salt in a food processor until well combined. Remove the dough to a lightly floured surface. Knead until firm and smooth, adding the 2 tablespoons flour if necessary to prevent sticking. Wrap the dough in plastic wrap. Refrigerate for 1 hour.

RAVIOLI FILLING: Toss the radicchio with the oil. Grill or broil 2 minutes on each side. Finely chop enough grilled radicchio to measure 1/2 cup. Combine radicchio, ricotta cheese, mozzarella cheese, egg, shallot, garlic, salt, pepper, parsley and lemon thyme in a bowl. Mix until well combined; set aside.

ASSEMBLY: Divide the dough in half. Wrap one half in plastic wrap. Roll out the other half in a pasta machine until setting #6 is reached. Scatter the parsley leaves over the surface of the pasta sheet. Fold the pasta sheet in half, encasing the parsley leaves inside. Roll the folded pasta sheet in the pasta machine until setting #6 is reached again. This is the top layer of pasta for the ravioli. Cover with plastic wrap and set aside. Roll the remaining dough until setting #6 is reached. Spoon 12 (2 1/2-tablespoon) portions of the filling over the surface of this second pasta sheet, spacing evenly. Combine the egg and water in a bowl. Brush egg mixture around the edges of pasta sheet. Place the parsley pasta sheet over the bottom sheet. Press all the way around the edges of the 2 sheets to seal. Cut out the ravioli using a 4-inch round cutter, making sure the filling is centered in each. Store the ravioli in a container dusted with semolina flour. Refrigerate until ready to cook. Bring 6 quarts salted water to a boil. Add the ravioli, stirring gently to separate. Return the water to a boil. Reduce the heat to medium. Cook for 8 to 10 minutes or until tender. Drain and serve immediately.

ROASTED TOMATO FENNEL SAUCE

4 pounds ripe tomatoes
Olive oil
Salt and pepper to taste
3 medium fennel bulbs
9 cloves of garlic, peeled
4 cups vegetable or chicken stock
   (preferably homemade)
1 1/2 teaspoons salt

MAKES 1 3/4 QUARTS

Cut the tomatoes in half. Rub with olive oil and sprinkle with salt and pepper. Trim off the tops and bottoms of the fennel bulbs. Cut each bulb lengthwise into eighths. Season with olive oil, salt and pepper. Toss the garlic cloves with olive oil. Place the tomatoes, fennel and garlic on a baking sheet. Bake at 450 degrees for 45 minutes or until golden brown. Peel the roasted tomatoes.

Transfer the roasted vegetables to a stockpot. Add the chicken stock. Bring to a boil; reduce the heat. Simmer until the fennel is tender. Process the mixture until puréed, using a handheld blender, food processor or blender; strain. Add 1 1/2 teaspoons salt and pepper to taste.

TRI-COLORED SALAD WITH BALSAMIC VINEGAR

1 bunch arugula
2 heads radicchio
1 head Belgian endive
1/2 cup aged balsamic vinegar
1/2 cup extra-virgin olive oil
Salt and cracked pepper to taste
1/2 cup (3-ounce block) shaved
   Parmesan cheese

SERVES 6 TO 8

Jack Simko brought me a bottle of 12-year balsamic vinegar from Boston as a "chef's gift." It was the inspiration for this salad.

L.A.R.

Trim off and discard the bottom of the arugula. Place the arugula in a large bowl of lukewarm water. Soak for 8 minutes. Drain well and rinse. Spin the leaves in a salad spinner; set aside. Remove the hearts of the radicchio and endive. Separate the leaves, rinse and spin-dry. Place the arugula, radicchio and endive in a large salad bowl. Whisk together the balsamic vinegar, oil, salt and pepper. Drizzle over the salad. Toss gently to combine. Top with the shaved Parmesan cheese.

An Experiment

When Anne Marie approached me with the idea of doing a Friday Night Dinner at the Inn, I remember being excited about the many possibilities. Things were quieting down for the catering season and the thought of preparing nourishing food for twenty-two guests was relaxing to my soul. After spending seven months in a bustling, energetic kitchen with up to fifteen wonderful co-workers, cooking for hundreds, I was looking forward to creating comforting food for an intimate group of Inn guests. Never did I dream it would become such a success!

People who arrived at the Inn late in the afternoon would wander into the kitchen and ask about the enticing aromas that were filling the air. "What's that incredible smell? What time is dinner?" These were the questions most asked by guests. Our guests were excited and so was I.

As couples entered the dining room for dinner, softly lit by elegant taper candles, our evening discussion would often begin with the topic of our selected wines and why they were a particularly good pairing for the evening meal. Guests were then invited to start with a salad, or, if they were of the European tradition, enjoy salad after the main meal.

As the evening progressed, a magical thing began to happen. The Sterns sitting at the table closest to the window were discussing the projected snowfall with the Scotts. The Morlands decided to share a table with the Thompsons and together they ordered a beautiful bottle of wine. Suddenly, the dining room was filled with conversation, smiles, laughter, and lots of warmth! It was a pleasure to be a part of this experience. By the time guests started to have dessert and coffee, I knew everyone by name and we were discussing what we were going to have for breakfast the next morning! The guests were now relaxed, the city was far behind, and everyone had discovered the magic of The Inn at the Round Barn Farm.

Leslie Rossetto

PORK CHOPS DELORES

Sunday afternoons were always a very special day in the Rossetto household. My father believed that with everyone's busy schedule, if we didn't sit down at the table together once a week to share a meal the family would break down completely. Our Sunday afternoon time together was very important to us all. Mom's pork chops were a favorite. The house smelled so good as they baked. We couldn't wait to sit down and take that first bite! Thanks, Mom, for all the nurturing food!

L.A.R.

2 eggs
1 cup seasoned Italian bread
 crumbs
4 pork loin chops, 1 inch thick
1 cup vegetable oil
¹/₂ cup dry white wine

SERVES 4

Beat the eggs in a shallow bowl. Place the bread crumbs in another shallow bowl. Dip the pork chops into the eggs, then into the bread crumbs, coating well. Heat the oil in a large skillet over medium-high heat until hot. Add the pork chops. Cook until golden brown on both sides. Drain on paper towels. Place the browned chops in a glass baking dish. Pour the wine into the dish. Bake, covered, at 350 degrees for 30 minutes. Turn the pork chops over. Bake, covered, for an additional 30 minutes. Uncover. Bake for 15 minutes. The total baking time is 1 hour and 15 minutes.

ALDO'S GARLIC CARROTS

One of my fondest memories as a child was back in 1966 when my father, Aldo, first made his garlic carrots. We had just moved into a new house and my dad immediately built a beautiful outdoor barbeque. I remember the first fire being built, the sight of his cast-iron pan, and the sizzle of thinly sliced carrots. When the garlic was added, the most amazing aroma filled the neighborhood. Dad, I can't thank you enough for giving me the gift of appreciating family, food, and friends.

L.A.R.

3 pounds carrots

12 cloves of garlic

2 tablespoons extra-virgin olive oil

Salt and pepper to taste

SERVES 6

Peel and diagonally slice enough carrots $^1/_8$ inch thick to measure about $4^1/_2$ cups. Peel and slice enough garlic cloves $^1/_{16}$ inch thick to measure $^3/_4$ cup. Heat the oil in a large skillet over medium heat until hot. Add the carrots. Sauté for 7 minutes or until tender and almost golden brown. Add the garlic slices. Sauté for 6 to 8 minutes or until the garlic and carrots are an even golden brown. Season with salt and pepper and cook for 1 more minute.

ARUGULA MASHED POTATOES

This is a new twist on an old favorite. The Inn guests went wild for this one.

L.A.R.

1 bunch (1 cup) arugula

3 pounds russet or Idaho potatoes, peeled and cut into quarters

$^1/_2$ cup unsalted butter

2 teaspoons salt

$^1/_3$ cup half-and-half, warmed

SERVES 6

Trim off and discard the bottom of the arugula. Place the arugula in a large bowl of lukewarm water. Soak for 8 minutes. Drain well and rinse. Spin the leaves in a salad spinner; finely chop the arugula and set aside. Cook the potatoes in boiling water until tender. Drain. Return the potatoes to the saucepan. Add the butter, salt and warm half-and-half. Mash well. Fold the arugula into the mashed potatoes.

PORTOBELLO WELLINGTON WITH BOURSIN CHEESE

This is an elegant and delicious entrée that we serve as a vegetarian option for our Friday night winter dinners. It can also be served as an appetizer.

L.A.R.

MUSHROOMS

1/2 cup olive oil

2 tablespoons lemon juice

1/4 cup chopped fresh parsley

2 teaspoons chopped fresh basil

4 cloves of garlic, minced

8 medium portobello mushrooms, stems removed

1 1/2 cups vegetable stock or wine

BOURSIN CHEESE

8 ounces cream cheese, softened

1/4 cup chopped fresh basil leaves

1 tablespoon chopped fresh parsley

1 tablespoon minced garlic

1 tablespoon half-and-half

Salt and pepper to taste

ASSEMBLY

1 sheet (1/2 of 17-ounce package) frozen puff pastry, thawed

1 egg

1 tablespoon water

SERVES 4

MUSHROOMS: Combine the olive oil, lemon juice, parsley, basil and garlic in a bowl. Brush the oil mixture over the mushrooms. Heat a cast-iron skillet over high heat until hot. Brush the skillet with olive oil. Add the mushrooms, cap sides down. Sear for 4 to 5 minutes. Turn the mushrooms over. Cook until softened and a rich golden brown, adding liquid as needed to the pan to prevent burning. Drain the mushrooms on paper towels.

BOURSIN CHEESE: Process the cream cheese, basil, parsley and garlic in a food processor until well blended. Add the half-and-half. Process to blend. Season with salt and pepper. (The leftover boursin cheese makes a delicious dip. Refrigerate, covered, for up to 1 week.)

ASSEMBLY: Roll out the puff pastry sheet to a 9-inch square on a lightly floured board. Cut the square into 4 squares measuring 4 1/2 inches each. Place 4 mushrooms, bottom side up, on each pastry square. Place 2 tablespoons of Boursin cheese in each mushroom. Place the remaining mushrooms on top. Combine the egg and water in a bowl. Brush the egg mixture around the edges of each pastry square. Bring the opposite corners of each square together and pinch to seal. Pinch the pastry seams to completely enclose the mushrooms. Brush the top of each pastry bundle with egg mixture. Place the bundles on an ungreased baking sheet. Bake at 400 degrees for about 20 minutes or until puffed and golden brown. Note: If you have extra puff pastry, roll out and cut into decorative shapes, such as stars or hearts. Spread one side of the cutouts with egg mixture and place on centers of bundles before baking.

LESLIE'S KEY LIME PIE WITH VERMONT MAPLE SYRUP AND WHIPPED CREAM

After visiting my sister and her family in Florida, I arrived back in Vermont with a bucketful of Key limes and decided that the upcoming Friday night dessert would be Key Lime Pie. I asked Richard, our resident innkeeper, to pick up two cans of sweetened condensed milk for the pies. He returned to the Inn and I quickly whipped up the pies, put them in the oven and continued on with the rest of my dinner preparations. While the guests were finishing up their dinners, I went to the kitchen and tested the pie. I cut into one of the pies, took a small bite, and discovered a huge problem. My lips smacked together faster than I could say evaporated milk instead of sweetened condensed milk! We had a little kitchen meeting and decided that this tart Key Lime Pie would be nice served in a pool of Vermont maple syrup and topped with whipped cream. We tried it, we loved it, and so did the guests. So always remember, when life gives you lemons, make lemonade!

L.A.R.

1¹/₂ cups graham cracker crumbs

3 tablespoons sugar

3 tablespoons unsalted butter, melted

10 egg yolks

2 (14-ounce) cans evaporated milk

1¹/₂ cups Key lime juice

Vermont maple syrup

Whipped cream

1 lime or lemon, cut into wedges (optional)

MAKES 1 (9-INCH) PIE

Combine the graham cracker crumbs, sugar and melted butter in a bowl. Press into the bottom and up the side of a 9-inch pie plate. Bake at 325 degrees for 10 minutes. Remove and set aside. Whisk together the egg yolks and evaporated milk in a large bowl until smooth. Add the Key lime juice and mix well. Pour the lime mixture into the baked pie shell. Bake at 325 degrees for 20 minutes. Cool. Refrigerate, covered, for at least 4 hours before serving. Pour a small pool of maple syrup on each dessert plate. Top with a slice of pie. Pipe a rosette of whipped cream on the plate next to the pie. Garnish with lime wedges.

The Morning Meal

Every morning I drive 1.2 miles from my home to the Inn. I think I am the only person in the world that wishes my commute were longer. Making the drive in the early morning hours, as the sun is just determining what its mood will be for the day, I realize why I am so at peace living here; I know why others travel to this magical Valley.

This morning as I sit and write this chapter opener, the skies and mountains are covered with what many locals call Sugarbush Pink—a rich hue of rose, purple, gray, and amber that softly cascades over the mountains. The colors that come with the rising sun respect the strong mountains. Within minutes, the spectacle is over and the day has begun. Lucky are the guests who can get themselves out of the safe haven of their down-covered beds to take a morning walk up the East Warren Road to the crest of the hill to enjoy this spiritual beauty. Subtle in their lusciousness, Vermont mornings are not boisterous.

Our mornings in the kitchen at The Inn at the Round Barn Farm usually start about 7:00 a.m. We try to prepare as many elements of the morning meal as possible the day before, so we can be at ease in our kitchen as guests are starting to come down for their first cup of coffee and morning chat. I personally have been accused of being able to cook breakfast in my sleep and showing up at the very last minute in which it is still possible to create a wonderful breakfast for twenty-two guests. And I admit, there is a lot of truth to that accusation. And for any guest that has ever come down to breakfast half asleep, an awakening happens between the fruit and baked goods course!

We cherish the morning meal at our Inn. It is truly the only opportunity an innkeeper of a Bed and Breakfast has to show off skills in the kitchen and nourish guests with food. You'll find the following recipes simple yet elegant, and foolproof. We have been making these throughout the years, and are not yet bored making the "same ol' thing." Each season allows us to garnish a dish differently, or change one ingredient to put a seasonal touch to an old standard. Feel free to adapt all but one of these recipes. My Cottage Cheese Pancakes with Raspberry Maple Syrup is sacred!

A.M.D.

THE MORNING MEAL

Vermont Maple Baked Pears

Cantaloupe Carousels with Toasted Walnuts,
Honey and Ricotta Filling

Annie's Vermont Baked Apples

Grand Marnier Citrus Cocktail

Truly the Best Blueberry Muffins

Rhubarb Streusel Muffins

Ginger Peach Muffins

Maple Butter

Dried Cranberry, Buttermilk, Oatmeal Scones

Light-As-A-Feather Blueberry Waffles

Cottage Cheese Pancakes with Raspberry Maple Syrup

Pumpkin Soufflé Pancakes with Hot Apple Compote

Luscious Lemon-Blueberry Pancakes

Overnight Salsa Soufflé

Scrumptious Banana Bread Pudding

Round Barn Fruit-Drenched French Toast

Maple Sausage and Apple Morning Torta

*Caramelized Leeks, Vermont Ham
and Brie Breakfast "Sammies"*

Garden Vegetable Hash

VERMONT MAPLE BAKED PEARS

his is my original baked pear recipe. In my opinion, maple flavoring is not limited to any season. While cooking breakfast one morning, Annie decided to add some cranberry juice to the baking dish, giving these pears a wonderful fall twist and vibrant color. I still stick to my traditional ways and always pair this fruit with a savory breakfast entrée.

A.M.D.

¹/₄ cup butter, softened

2 tablespoons granulated sugar

4 very ripe pears (Bartlett, Comice or any type that is ripe and in season)

Vermont maple syrup

Brown sugar

Allspice

Raisins

Heavy cream (optional)

SERVES 4

Rub the butter over the bottom of an 8x8-inch baking dish, coating well. Leave any remaining butter in the dish. Dust the buttered dish with the granulated sugar. Peel the pears. Trim a sliver off the bottom of each pear so that it stands upright. Place in the prepared dish. Drizzle the tops of the pears with maple syrup. Sprinkle with brown sugar and allspice. Add the desired amount of raisins to the bottom of the dish. Bake at 325 degrees for 15 minutes. (The juices from the pears will mix with the butter and sugars to create a caramel coating.) Serve the pears on individual dishes. Spoon the juices and raisins over and top with a splash of heavy cream. Garnish with fresh pansies.

CANTALOUPE CAROUSELS

1 ripe cantaloupe
1¹/2 cups ricotta cheese
2 tablespoons honey
¹/4 cup chopped toasted walnuts
2 tablespoons raisins
Grape clusters
Strawberries
Freshly grated nutmeg

SERVES 4 TO 6

Peel the cantaloupe by cutting off each end, then cutting down the side of the melon from top to bottom around the entire fruit. Cut the melon crosswise into 1-inch slices to form rings, removing the seeds. (There will be 4 to 6 rings depending on the size of the melon.) Combine the ricotta cheese and honey in a mixing bowl. Fold the walnuts and raisins in gently. Place each melon ring on a plate. Fill the center of each ring with a spoonful of the ricotta mixture. Garnish with the grapes, strawberries and a dusting of nutmeg.

ANNIE'S VERMONT BAKED APPLES

My father has always called me Annie. He is a lover of apples and together we have perfected this baked apple. When cooking breakfast in the kitchen together, we still differ on how soft the cooked apple should be. This is a wonderful presentation without a lot of fuss.

A.M.D.

4 McIntosh or Northern Spy apples
¹/4 cup butter, melted
¹/2 cup finely chopped pecans
2 cups apple juice, cranberry juice or apple cider
¹/2 cup raisins or fresh cranberries
Freshly grated nutmeg
¹/2 cup whipped cream

SERVES 4

Core the apples and remove the peel about ¹/3 of the way down from the tops. Dip the peeled parts of the apples into the melted butter, then roll in the pecans. Place the apples, nut sides up, in an 8x8-inch baking dish. Add the apple juice and raisins to the dish, making sure the raisins are submersed in the juice to prevent burning. Sprinkle the tops of the apples with nutmeg. Bake at 350 degrees for 20 minutes or until the apples pop out of their skins a bit. (Do not bake too long or you will have applesauce.) Serve topped with whipped cream and garnished with a sliver of cinnamon stick.

GRAND MARNIER CITRUS COCKTAIL

5 oranges
1 cup water
1/2 cup granulated sugar
1 lime
Brown sugar
4 teaspoons Grand Marnier, or
     to taste

SERVES 4

Our citrus "cocktail" adds a touch of elegance to the morning fruit course. The hint of Grand Marnier combined with a lovely presentation in a sugar-rimmed antique crystal goblet sets the stage for a special day.

K.A.M.

Remove the orange peel in strips from 1 of the oranges using a vegetable peeler or citrus stripper, being careful not to remove too much of the white pith. Cut the orange peel into about 2-inch lengths; cut into very fine julienne strips. Bring the water to a boil in a saucepan. Add the granulated sugar and orange peel. Boil gently for 4 minutes. Remove from the heat and let cool. Drain and set aside.

Slice off both ends of the remaining 4 oranges. Cut down the sides of the oranges from top to bottom with a sharp knife to completely remove the peel and white pith. Remove the individual orange sections by first cutting on 1 side of each section membrane and then on the other. Keep cutting around the oranges until all of the sections have been removed; set aside.

Remove the zest from the lime; set aside. Place some brown sugar in a bowl large enough to hold the rim of the goblets or glasses you plan to use for serving. Slice the lime. Moisten the rims of the goblets with the lime slices. Dip the rims into the brown sugar to coat.

Distribute the orange sections among the goblets. Top each with 1 teaspoon Grand Marnier. Garnish with the reserved candied orange peel and lime zest.

TRULY THE BEST BLUEBERRY MUFFINS

Everyone loves blueberry muffins! This one makes our morning a bit more relaxed because we have found that the batter is perfect for baking when it has been refrigerated overnight.

A.M.D.

6 tablespoons butter, softened

1¼ cups sugar

2 eggs

2 cups flour

2 teaspoons baking powder

½ teaspoon salt

½ cup milk

1 pint (2 cups) blueberries

4 teaspoons sugar, divided

2 teaspoons flour

¼ teaspoon cinnamon

MAKES 12 MUFFINS

Cream the butter and 1¼ cups sugar in a mixer bowl until very light and fluffy. Add the eggs. Beat for 2 minutes. Combine the 2 cups flour, baking powder and salt in a bowl. Add to the butter mixture alternately with the milk. Place the blueberries in a bowl. Sprinkle with 2 teaspoons sugar and 2 teaspoons flour. Toss gently. Fold the blueberries gently into the batter just until blended. Refrigerate, covered, overnight. Spoon the batter into 12 greased muffin cups, filling almost to the top. Combine the remaining 2 teaspoons sugar and cinnamon in a bowl. Sprinkle over the tops of the muffins. Bake at 375 degrees for 25 minutes or until golden brown.

RHUBARB STREUSEL MUFFINS

One of our very special employees, Jennifer McDermott, submitted this recipe to Cooking Light *magazine and they adapted it to the light version that follows.*

A.M.D.

1 1/4 cups firmly packed brown
    sugar

1 cup buttermilk

1/2 cup vegetable oil

1 egg

2 teaspoons vanilla extract

1 1/2 cups diced rhubarb

2 1/2 cups flour

1 teaspoon baking soda

1 teaspoon baking powder

1/2 teaspoon salt

1/2 cup granulated sugar

1/2 cup chopped nuts (your choice)

1 tablespoon butter, melted

2 teaspoons cinnamon

MAKES 12 MUFFINS

Combine the brown sugar, buttermilk, oil, egg and vanilla in a large bowl. Add the rhubarb. Stir together the flour, baking soda, baking powder and salt in a bowl. Add the flour mixture to the rhubarb mixture. Stir until blended. Spoon the batter into 12 greased muffin cups, filling 2/3 full. Combine the granulated sugar, nuts, butter and cinnamon in a bowl. Sprinkle over the tops of the muffins. Bake at 400 degrees for 20 to 25 minutes or until golden brown.

NOTE: You may substitute other fruit for the rhubarb. Our favorite is raspberries!

LIGHTER VERSION: Use 1 cup brown sugar, 1/4 cup oil, 1/2 teaspoon vanilla extract and 1 3/4 cups flour. For topping, use 2 tablespoons quick-cooking oats, 1/4 cup sugar, 3 tablespoons butter and 2 teaspoons cinnamon.

GINGER PEACH MUFFINS

There is nothing like a delicate peach muffin. These are great in the summer made with fresh peaches and just as good in the winter with frozen peaches. The Raspberry Maple Butter (below) makes them sublime!

A.R.R.

1 cup sugar, divided
3 tablespoons grated gingerroot
1 tablespoon grated lemon zest
    (1 lemon)
1/2 cup unsalted butter, softened
2 eggs, room temperature
1 cup buttermilk
2 cups flour
3/4 teaspoon baking soda
1/2 teaspoon salt
1 cup chopped fresh or frozen
    peaches

MAKES 12 MUFFINS

Heat 1/4 cup of the sugar and the gingerroot in a small saucepan over medium heat, stirring until the sugar is dissolved. Cool. Stir in the lemon zest; set aside. Cream the butter and remaining 3/4 cup sugar in a bowl until well mixed. Add the eggs and beat well. Add the buttermilk and mix until combined. Combine the flour, baking soda and salt in bowl. Add the flour mixture to the butter mixture. Stir just until combined. Fold in the ginger mixture and peaches. Spoon the batter into 12 greased muffin cups, filling 3/4 full. Bake at 375 degrees for 20 to 25 minutes or until golden brown.

VARIATION: Substitute blueberries or raspberries for the peaches.

MAPLE BUTTER

1 cup butter, softened
2 tablespoons maple syrup
1 teaspoon cinnamon

MAKES 1 CUP

Beat the butter, maple syrup and cinnamon in a mixer bowl until smooth. (Or, process the ingredients in a food processor until smooth.)

VARIATIONS:

RASPBERRY MAPLE BUTTER: add 1 tablespoon all-fruit raspberry jam.

STRAWBERRY MAPLE BUTTER: add 1 tablespoon all-fruit strawberry jam.

DRIED CRANBERRY, BUTTERMILK, OATMEAL SCONES

Like the time I have spent in my mission to find the ultimate chocolate chip cookie, I have also spent a great deal of my life looking for the ultimate scone. Kate Mahoney, the Inn's permanent part-time Assistant Innkeeper and chief recipe tester, has created it!

A.M.D.

SCONES

3 cups plus 2 tablespoons flour

$^1/_2$ cup plus 2 tablespoons sugar

$2^1/_2$ teaspoons baking powder

$1^1/_4$ teaspoons baking soda

$1^1/_4$ teaspoons salt

$1^1/_4$ cups cold unsalted butter, cut into $^1/_4$-inch pieces

2 cups rolled oats

1 cup dried cranberries

2 tablespoons finely chopped orange zest

$^3/_4$ cup buttermilk

GLAZE

2 teaspoons sugar

1 teaspoon cinnamon

1 teaspoon heavy cream

MAKES 16 SCONES

SCONES: Combine the flour, sugar, baking powder, baking soda and salt in the bowl of an electric mixer. Add the butter. Mix on low speed until the butter is the size of small peas. Add the oats, cranberries and orange zest. Mix on low speed while slowly pouring in the buttermilk. Mix just until the dough comes together. Gather the dough into a ball and divide in half. Roll out each half to a $^3/_4$- to 1-inch-thick circle on a lightly floured board. Cut each circle into 8 wedges. Place the scones on a parchment-paper-lined baking sheet. Bake at 350 degrees for 22 to 24 minutes or until golden brown.

GLAZE: Combine the sugar, cinnamon and cream in a small bowl. Brush the glaze over the scones while they are still warm.

Waffle Secrets

My oldest brother John and I are very close. When the Inn was first opened, he and his wife Kathy came to stay as "guests." I was so excited to prepare breakfast for them. As I stood in the kitchen making waffle batter, John entered the room and asked what I was planning on serving for breakfast. I proudly told him waffles. There was no response. When I questioned my brother about his lack of enthusiasm, he simply and cautiously asked, "Are they like Mom's waffles?"

My mother had five children within six years. She is a saint. From grammar school to high school, she got up each and every school morning and made a full, hot, cooked breakfast for all of her children. She never skipped a day, but we often tried to skip out on her waffles. At that moment in the kitchen, John and I shared a hidden secret . . . my mother's waffles were the worst! Dry, flat, and tasteless, even Vermont's best maple syrup couldn't help them. John and I then insisted that the problem must have been with her vintage waffle iron.

My brother's "waffle secret," coupled with my mother's devotion to serving her family a hot, healthy breakfast, has been an inspiration to me throughout the years. Waffles are now a specialty of the Inn, and we are constantly creating moist, fluffy, and flavor-filled mouthwatering combinations of this old-time standard.

A.M.D.

LIGHT-AS-A-FEATHER BLUEBERRY WAFFLES

3 eggs, separated
1 1/2 cups half-and-half
1/2 cup butter, melted
1 1/2 cups flour
1 tablespoon granulated sugar
2 teaspoons baking powder
1/2 teaspoon salt
1 cup fresh or frozen blueberries
Confectioners' sugar

MAKES 10 SINGLE BELGIAN WAFFLES

The waffles story on page 59 tells all! Someday I'll publish a cookbook just on waffles.

A.M.D.

Beat the egg whites in the large bowl of an electric mixer until stiff peaks form; set aside. Beat the egg yolks in a large bowl with a hand mixer until light yellow in color. Blend in the half-and-half and melted butter.

Sift together the flour, granulated sugar, baking powder and salt. Mix into the egg yolk mixture until combined. Fold 1/4 of the beaten egg whites into the batter to lighten it. Fold in the blueberries and remaining egg whites just until combined. Preheat a Belgian waffle iron. Grease the waffle iron with nonstick cooking spray just before using. Pour 1/2 cup batter onto each side of the hot waffle iron. Bake according to the manufacturer's instructions. (In a good professional Belgian waffle iron, the waffles are done in only 45 seconds.) Repeat the process until all the batter is used. Sprinkle the waffles with confectioners' sugar. Serve with butter and maple syrup.

VARIATION: Raspberries may be substituted for the blueberries.

COTTAGE CHEESE PANCAKES WITH RASPBERRY MAPLE SYRUP

This is the most requested recipe at the Inn. When checking guests into the Inn, we try to tell everyone what's on the menu for breakfast. We keep the cottage cheese a secret until after guests have had their first bite of these pancakes.

A.M.D.

COTTAGE CHEESE PANCAKES

1 cup large curd cottage cheese
4 eggs
1/2 cup flour
1/4 cup butter, melted

RASPBERRY MAPLE SYRUP

1 cup Vermont maple syrup
2/3 cup fresh or frozen raspberries
2 tablespoons raspberry jam

MAKES 12 (4-INCH) PANCAKES

COTTAGE CHEESE PANCAKES: Beat the cottage cheese in a bowl with an electric mixer until it appears whipped. Add the eggs and flour and mix until the wet and dry ingredients are combined. With the mixer running, add the melted butter. (This should form a thick batter. Test a small amount of batter on a hot greased griddle or skillet. If the batter seems too thin, stir in a small amount of flour to thicken.) Spoon 1/4 cup batter for each pancake onto a hot greased griddle or skillet. Bake until golden. Flip the pancakes and bake the other side for 1 minute. Do not overcook. The pancakes should be moist and spring back to the touch. Serve with Raspberry Maple Syrup.

RASPBERRY MAPLE SYRUP: Combine the maple syrup and raspberries in a nonstick saucepan. Cook over low heat until heated through, stirring occasionally. Stir in the jam. Heat until the syrup mixture boils. Remove from the heat and let stand for a few minutes to thicken before spooning over the pancakes.

NOTE: Grade B dark amber maple syrup has the best flavor for cooking.

PUMPKIN SOUFFLÉ PANCAKES WITH HOT APPLE COMPOTE

When misty summer mornings start to give way to days that start with a nip in the air . . . these perfect fall pancakes make their way onto the Round Barn griddle.

A.M.D.

PUMPKIN PANCAKES

1 cup milk

2/3 cup pumpkin

2 eggs

1/3 cup vegetable oil

1/2 teaspoon vanilla extract

1 cup flour

2 teaspoons baking powder

1/2 teaspoon cinnamon

1/2 teaspoon allspice

1/2 teaspoon nutmeg

APPLE COMPOTE

1/4 cup butter

6 tart apples, peeled, cored and sliced 1/2 inch thick

1/4 cup apple cider, apple juice or water

1/4 cup sugar

Zest of 1 lemon

1 teaspoon grated gingerroot (optional)

MAKES 12 (4-INCH) PANCAKES AND ABOUT 5 CUPS COMPOTE

PUMPKIN PANCAKES: Combine the milk, pumpkin, eggs, oil and vanilla in a large bowl. Combine the flour, baking powder, cinnamon, allspice and nutmeg in a bowl. Slowly stir the flour mixture into the pumpkin mixture until well blended. Spoon 1/3 cup batter for each pancake onto a medium-hot greased griddle or skillet. Bake for 3 to 4 minutes per side. Do not flip the pancakes over until the edges are firm or they will fall apart. Serve with hot apple compote.

APPLE COMPOTE: Melt the butter in a sauté pan. Combine the apples, apple cider, sugar, lemon zest and gingerroot in the prepared pan. Cook, covered, over medium heat for 15 minutes or until the apples are soft, but still firm. The apple compote is also a great topping for French toast and other types of pancakes, as well as a filling for apple strudel.

VARIATION: Add 1/2 cup dried cranberries for a beautiful contrast.

LUSCIOUS LEMON-BLUEBERRY PANCAKES

These pancakes, originally from the Four Seasons Hotel but adapted by countless others, are to die for. Next to Anne Marie's Cottage Cheese Pancakes (page 61), these are one of my absolute favorites. They are as light as clouds and melt in your mouth.

A.R.R.

³/4 cup ricotta cheese

3 eggs, separated

¹/4 cup unsalted butter, melted

¹/2 teaspoon vanilla extract

2 teaspoons lemon extract

¹/4 cup flour

2 tablespoons sugar

Zest of 2 lemons, finely grated

¹/8 teaspoon salt

1 cup frozen Maine or other small blueberries

MAKES 10 (3-INCH) PANCAKES

Beat the ricotta cheese, egg yolks, butter, vanilla and lemon extract in a medium bowl until well mixed. Combine the flour, sugar, lemon zest and salt in a small bowl and mix well. Stir the flour mixture into the ricotta mixture, mixing carefully. Whip the egg whites in a clean, dry medium bowl until stiff peaks form. Mix a small amount of the beaten egg whites into the batter with a rubber spatula. Fold the remaining egg whites in carefully, using as few strokes as possible. Spoon ¹/4 cup batter for each pancake onto a hot, lightly greased griddle or skillet. Sprinkle a few frozen blueberries on the surface of each pancake. Bake until golden brown. Flip the pancakes when small bubbles appear on the tops and the bottoms are firm. Bake until golden brown. Serve immediately or keep warm in a 200-degree oven.

VARIATION: Omit the blueberries and increase the lemon zest by 1 teaspoon for lipsmacking lemony pancakes. Serve with Raspberry Maple Syrup (page 61).

OVERNIGHT SALSA SOUFFLÉ

This egg, milk, and bread recipe, also called "Eggs with a Kick," has many variations. Try hash brown potatoes and herbs instead of the pepper, mushrooms, and tomato salsa-like combination, or sausage, maple syrup, and apple; or bacon and tomato. Wonderful for those who really aren't early risers but want to make an impressive presentation at breakfast!

A.M.D.

1 loaf French bread, cut into
    1-inch cubes
1/2 cup chopped red bell pepper
1/2 cup chopped green bell pepper
1/3 cup sliced fresh mushrooms
1 tablespoon butter
1/2 cup crumbled feta cheese
3 cups milk
10 eggs
1 teaspoon finely chopped fresh dill
10 tomato slices
1 cup shredded sharp Cheddar
    cheese

SERVES 10

Place the bread cubes in a greased 9x13-inch baking dish. (The dish should be 3/4 full.) Sauté the red pepper, green pepper and mushrooms in the butter in a skillet until tender. Spread the vegetables evenly over the bread. Sprinkle the feta cheese over the vegetables.

    Combine the milk, eggs and dill in a bowl until well blended. Pour the egg mixture over the bread, making sure all the bread is moistened. Arrange the tomato slices on top, placing a slice in the center of each of what will be 10 portions, with 5 slices down and 2 across. Sprinkle with the Cheddar cheese. Cover the dish with a piece of greased foil, greased side down. Refrigerate overnight. Bake, covered, at 350 degrees for 50 to 60 minutes or until firm in the center. Let stand for 10 minutes before serving.

SCRUMPTIOUS BANANA BREAD PUDDING

We serve this for breakfast but the leftovers served with vanilla ice cream are my mother's favorite treat for a late-night snack.

A.M.D.

¹/₂ cup butter, softened

¹/₃ cup peach or raspberry preserves

1 loaf sliced white bread

3 to 4 ripe bananas

Lemon juice

4 cups half-and-half

4 eggs

¹/₃ cup sugar

2 teaspoons vanilla extract

1 teaspoon cinnamon

¹/₂ teaspoon nutmeg

SERVES 10 TO 12

Combine the butter and preserves in a bowl. Spread 1 side of each bread slice with the butter mixture. Slice the bananas thinly and dip each slice in lemon juice to prevent browning. Place the bananas on the buttered sides of half of the bread slices. Top with the remaining bread slices, buttered sides down, forming sandwiches. (If you like to plan ahead or are using this for company, the banana sandwiches may be prepared the night before, covered and refrigerated.)

Slice the banana sandwiches in half diagonally. Combine the half-and-half, eggs, sugar, vanilla, cinnamon and nutmeg in a large mixing bowl. Dip the sandwich halves into the egg mixture. Arrange in a greased 9x13-inch baking dish, overlapping slightly. Pour any remaining egg mixture over the sandwiches in the dish. Set the baking dish in a larger pan and place on the rack of a 350-degree oven. Pour hot water into the larger pan so that it comes about halfway up the sides of the smaller baking dish, creating a hot water bath for the smaller pan. Bake for 35 to 45 minutes or until the bread is lightly browned and the center is set.

We serve this on a plate decorated with a swirl of raspberry purée and a dusting of confectioners' sugar. Our homemade sausage and a few fresh raspberries are a nice accompaniment.

ROUND BARN FRUIT-DRENCHED FRENCH TOAST

I hate mushy French toast! The cornflake coating allows me to prepare this in advance, leaving plenty of time for me to chat with my guests in the morning. When cooked, the flakes keep the French toast crisp on the outside and delicately moist on the inside. If summer fruits aren't available, use Winter Fruit Topping (below).

A.M.D.

1¹/2 cups milk

8 eggs

¹/2 cup heavy cream

1 tablespoon vanilla extract

Dash of freshly grated nutmeg

1 cup crushed cornflakes

12 (1-inch-thick) slices Italian
    bread

Assorted fresh summer fruits:
    strawberries, blueberries, sliced
    kiwifruit, bananas, peaches

Vermont maple syrup

Confectioners' sugar

WINTER FRUIT TOPPING

¹/4 cup butter

¹/2 cup packed dark brown sugar

1 (16-ounce) can sliced peaches
    with juice

1 cup fresh cranberries

1 to 2 bananas, sliced ¹/2 inch thick

SERVES 6

Whisk the milk, eggs and cream in a large bowl for 3 to 4 minutes or until well combined. (This allows the heavy cream to almost "whip" for a light batter.) Stir in the vanilla. Pour through a strainer to remove any excess egg. Stir the nutmeg into the strained mixture. Place the crushed cornflakes in a shallow bowl. Dip each bread slice into the egg mixture (do not oversoak), then dip 1 side into the cornflakes. (The prepared French toast slices can sit at room temperature for 30 to 45 minutes until guests are ready to eat.) Bake the French toast on a hot greased griddle, cornflake sides down first, until golden brown on both sides. Place 2 slices on each serving plate and top with fresh fruit, maple syrup and a dusting of confectioners' sugar.

WINTER FRUIT TOPPING: Melt the butter in a nonstick saucepan. Stir in the brown sugar until melted. Add the undrained peaches and cranberries. Bring to a boil; reduce the heat. Simmer gently for 20 minutes. Gently stir in the banana slices about 5 minutes before the French toast is ready to be served. Spoon the warm fruit over the French toast just before serving. If there are any leftovers, this fruit topping is great served over vanilla ice cream.

Maple Sausage and Apple Torta

Annie came home from the Essex Retreat Center in Massachusetts one Monday and said that she had just found a great new "do ahead" breakfast dish that featured my favorite combination of sausage and apples. We used my homemade sausage and added some Vermont maple syrup to bring this recipe closer to home.

A.M.D.

MAPLE SAUSAGE

1 pound ground pork
3 tablespoons Vermont maple syrup
1 teaspoon salt
1/2 teaspoon sage
1/2 teaspoon cardamom
1/4 teaspoon black pepper
1/4 teaspoon ginger
1/8 teaspoon dillweed
1/8 teaspoon mace

TORTA

3/4 pound Maple Sausage
1 1/2 cups chopped peeled apples
1 tablespoon butter
2 1/4 cups milk
6 eggs
1/3 cup Vermont maple syrup
1 teaspoon nutmeg
16 to 20 (1/2-inch-thick) slices
   French bread

SERVES 8 TO 10

MAPLE SAUSAGE: Combine the pork, maple syrup, salt, sage, cardamom, pepper, ginger, dillweed and mace in a bowl, stirring until thoroughly blended.

TORTA: Preheat the oven to 350 degrees. Brown the Maple Sausage in a skillet, stirring until crumbly; drain and set aside. Sauté the apples in the butter in a skillet until tender. Remove from the heat. Stir in the cooked sausage. Combine the milk, eggs, maple syrup and nutmeg in a bowl, mixing well. Grease a 9-inch springform pan. Cover the bottom of the pan on the outside with foil to prevent leaking. Dip 8 to 10 bread slices into the egg mixture and arrange them, overlapping and with no space between them, on the bottom of the prepared pan. Spoon the sausage and apple mixture on top of the bread. Dip 8 to 10 more bread slices into the egg mixture and arrange them, overlapping, over the sausage mixture. Pour any remaining egg mixture over the top and press down slightly. (The torta may be prepared in advance up to this point. Refrigerate, covered, overnight.) Bake, uncovered, at 350 degrees for 1 hour or until a knife inserted in the center comes out clean and the top is golden brown. Cut into pie-shaped wedges to serve.

This is best served with a creation by our chef Michael Forest fondly known as maple syrup apple "jamueli." Combine maple syrup, diced apples, and a cinnamon stick and simmer for 20 minutes. Spoon over the torta.

CARAMELIZED LEEKS, VERMONT HAM AND BRIE BREAKFAST "SAMMIES"

One afternoon Kate and I were looking for a new breakfast dish that could be served with traditional scrambled eggs. The Jones Dairy Company had just done a big promotion with the bed and breakfast industry and published a cookbook of new recipes that featured Jones Dairy products. We adapted a breakfast sandwich by Laura Simoes, owner of the Inn at Maplewood Farms in New Hampshire, to our Vermont version, using the local doughnut company's oatmeal bread, thinly sliced Vermont ham, and lots of Love. Thanks, Laura, for the original inspiration!

A.M.D.

2 large leeks, halved lengthwise, rinsed thoroughly and sliced 1/4 inch thick
1 tablespoon butter
3 tablespoons Vermont maple syrup
4 ounces Brie cheese, sliced
1/4 pound thinly sliced Vermont baked ham
8 thick slices oatmeal bread
4 tablespoons butter, softened

MAKES 4 SANDWICHES

Sauté the leeks in 1 tablespoon butter in a skillet for 4 to 5 minutes. Add the maple syrup. Simmer until tender and slightly caramelized. To create sandwiches, layer 1 ounce Brie cheese, 2 ham slices and 1/4 of the leeks on each of 4 bread slices. Top with the remaining bread slices. Spread 1 tablespoon softened butter on the outside of each sandwich. Cook on a heated griddle or skillet until the bread is toasted on both sides and the cheese is melted.

We like to slice these sandwiches diagonally into quarters, serving a half sandwich with a side of scrambled eggs and fresh sliced fruit to each person.

GARDEN VEGETABLE HASH

Amanda Gallant interned with Cooking from the Heart Catering and The Round Barn Farm during the summer of 1996. We had some great mornings in the kitchen and she brought this vegetable hash recipe to the Inn. Now a graduate of the New England Culinary Institute, Amanda lives in the state of Maine.

A.M.D.

1¼ pounds small red potatoes,
    cut into ¼-inch pieces
½ pound carrots, peeled and
    cut into ¼-inch pieces
1 large onion, chopped
2½ teaspoons olive oil
2 teaspoons butter
1 tablespoon chopped fresh thyme,
    divided
1 tablespoon chopped fresh
    rosemary, divided
2 red bell peppers, diced into
    ¼-inch pieces
½ pound asparagus, cut into
    ¼-inch pieces
1 cup vegetable stock or water
2 teaspoons each salt and pepper

SERVES 6 TO 8 (7 CUPS)

Place the potatoes in a saucepan of cold water. Bring to a boil; reduce the heat. Simmer for 5 minutes. Add the carrots and cook with the potatoes until the potatoes and carrots are tender; drain. Sauté the onion in the oil and butter in a nonstick pan until tender. Stir in 1½ teaspoons thyme, 1½ teaspoons rosemary, potatoes, peppers and carrots, mixing well. Cook until the potatoes have a golden crust. Add the asparagus, remaining 1½ teaspoons each thyme and rosemary and the vegetable stock. Cook until the stock reduces slightly and thickens, and the asparagus is tender. Add salt and pepper and cook for 2 more minutes. Adjust seasonings. Garnish with sliced green onions.

Growth of a Business...
Dreams Do Come True

*W*hen my parents and I opened this Inn, we had no idea to what extent our business would grow. We did know that we were going to have to sell more than just rooms to support a staff and keep us challenged. Our personalities are such that we are constantly challenging ourselves . . . sound like the definition of an entrepreneur?

In 1989, in the midst of our restoring the Joslyn Round Barn, a happily engaged couple walked into the Inn and innocently inquired when our barn was going to be finished. We honestly replied that we did not know. Getting a bit more specific, they asked if it was possibly going to be ready by the next August. We said possibly. Their dream was to get married in our barn. Many marriages have taken place on our grounds since theirs.

The most important marriage for me has not been the one of a bride and groom, but the marriage of two businesses. I knew that food at weddings was just as important as a beautiful facility. I also knew that I was not capable of providing a full menu of hors d'oeuvres and dinner for more than twenty-five people. But Annie Reed was.

In 1998, ten years after that first couple came inquiring, Annie Reed and I are now tried and true business partners and best friends. We "married" each other long before we became legal partners. And it's through this commitment and joint effort that we have been able to provide Vermont's best food and planning services to people here at the Round Barn and at many off-site catered events.

Our wedding business now accounts for more than one-third of our annual income. Our success in growing the wedding portion of our business is directly attributed to having a unique facility, never forgetting what customer service truly is, and exposing guests to fabulous catered food. I credit my father with the facility and grounds, my mother and all who have trained me for the service knowledge, and Cooking from the Heart Catering for the most-talked-about food ever provided for large events.

A.M.D.

The Inn at the Round Barn Farm and Cooking from the Heart Catering have provided services to brides and grooms, couples celebrating anniversaries and birthdays, businesses hosting parties and meetings, and families in need of a peaceful place to celebrate the life and mourn the loss of a loved one. Annie and I would like to remember Kitty Smyth in this chapter. Kitty was our calligrapher of handwritten menus offered through Cooking from the Heart Catering. We've included a sample of her talented work in memory of her, and thank her for providing one of those "special touches" we strive to find in our offerings.

A.M.D. and A.R.R.

Menu

Roasted Butternut Apple Soup with
Vermont Creme Fraiche

Salad of Baby Greens with edible
Flowers and Maple Balsamic Dressing

Choice of

Vermont Turkey stuffed with Apricot
Sage Dressing, Cranberry Compoté,
Roasted Garlic-Parsnip Dutchess
Potatoes and Melange of Seasonal
Vegetables

or

Salmon in Puffed Pastry with
Citrus Beurre Blanc Sauce, Wild
Rice Pilaf and Melange of
Seasonal Vegetables

Basket of Fresh Baked Breads

Wedding Cake

Coffee, Tea, Decaf

FRUIT, VEGETABLE AND CHEESE DISPLAY

Curried Mango Chutney Cheesecake with Toasted Coconut Crust

Artichoke, Spinach and Basil Dip

Roasted Meatballs in Blue Cheese Madeira Sauce

Black Bean Spirals with Fresh Tomato Salsa

Baked Brie in Puff Pastry with Jo Anna's Dried Cherry Chutney

American Flatbread • Fabulous Antipasto Presentation

Eggplant Caponata • Caramelized Onions

PASSED HORS D'OEUVRES

Miniature New England Crab Cakes with Chipotle Aioli Sauce

Lobster-Filled Phyllo Triangles Served with Sweet and Smoky Corn Relish

Vegetable Confetti Fritters with Roast Garlic Parmesan Dip

SIT-DOWN DINNER

Roasted Butternut Squash and Apple Soup with Ginger Crème Fraîche

Wild Rice Pancakes

Salmon Fillet in Puff Pastry with Citrus Beurre Blanc

A Modified Buffet

*Vermont Turkey Breast Stuffed with Fruited Cranberry-Sage
Dressing and Apple Cider Gravy*

Cranberry-Ginger Compote

*Grilled Loin of Pork Served with Red Onion Chutney
and Stephanie's Spiced Apples*

Oriental Vegetable Noodle Salad with Toasted Sesame Dressing

*Exotic Spinach Salad with Caramelized Onions, Mandarin Oranges,
Roasted Red Pepper and Shiitake Mushrooms Served
with Creamy Citrus Dressing*

Garlic Mashed Potatoes with Parsnip Purée

New England Corn Pudding

The Pasta Bar

Ravioli with Roasted Butternut Squash in Sage Pasta

Roasted Garlic Cream Sauce • Sage Brown Butter Sauce

Tomato-Basil Marinara • Southwest Pesto

Citrus Cream Sauce • Tomato Vodka Cream Sauce

Tuscan Al Fresca Sauce

CURRIED MANGO CHUTNEY CHEESECAKE

We probably get the most requests for this appetizer. It is also one recipe that I never get tired of. I made it up one day when I needed to bring an hors d'oeuvre to a party. To this day, I've never seen it in any other cookbook.

A.R.R.

CHEESECAKE

> 1 cup lightly toasted coconut, divided
> 16 ounces cream cheese, softened
> 1/2 cup mango chutney
> 2 eggs
> 1 green onion, white bulb and 1/2 inch of green top sliced
> 1 clove of garlic, minced
> 2 teaspoons curry powder
> 1 teaspoon salt

GARNISH

> 1/2 cup mango chutney
> 1 cup slivered almonds, toasted
> 1 cup sliced green onions
> 1/2 cup toasted flaked coconut
> 1/2 cup dried cranberries
> 1/2 cup golden raisins

SERVES 12

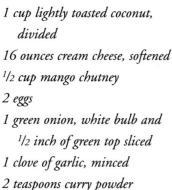

CHEESECAKE: Spread 1/2 cup coconut over the bottom of a buttered 7-inch springform pan; set aside. Beat the cream cheese in a mixer bowl or food processor until fluffy. Add the chutney, eggs, green onion, garlic, curry powder and salt and blend well. Spoon the cheese mixture into the prepared pan, spreading evenly. Bake at 300 degrees for 45 to 55 minutes or until firm. Refrigerate the cheesecake, uncovered, for 2 hours. Run a sharp knife along edges of the springform pan. Remove the cheesecake from the pan. Pat the remaining 1/2 cup coconut on the outside edge of the cheesecake.

GARNISH: Spread the top of the cheesecake with the chutney. Then choose one of the following decorating suggestions.

Sprinkle the almonds around the edge. Sprinkle the green onions in a circular fashion around the edge of the almonds. Sprinkle the coconut around the edge of the onions, forming 3 concentric circles.

Lightly score the top of the cheesecake into 10 equal wedges. Fill in each wedge with rows of dried cranberries, green onions, slivered almonds, golden raisins and coconut, repeating rows in same order until the wedge is filled in.

LIGHT VARIATION: Substitute light cream cheese and 1/2 cup egg substitute for the regular cream cheese and eggs.

NOTE: To fit a 9-inch springform pan that serves 20, double the recipe.

ARTICHOKE, SPINACH AND BASIL DIP

This recipe is dedicated to Dottie and John Ammerman who bring the Vermont Horse Show Festival to our valley each year. The show brings in a lot of extra business for all the shops, restaurants, and lodging, not to mention being a wonderful event to go and see. During this time, they host many parties, and this dip has become a standard requested favorite. Thank you, Dottie and John. We appreciate you!

A.R.R. and L.A.R.

5 ounces (about 4 cups) lightly
    packed fresh spinach leaves,
    cleaned and coarsely chopped
1 (14-ounce) can artichoke hearts,
    drained and coarsely chopped
$^1\!/_2$ cup chopped fresh basil leaves
$^1\!/_2$ cup mayonnaise
$^1\!/_2$ cup grated Romano or
    Parmesan cheese
2 cloves of garlic, minced
Black pepper to taste
Round bread loaf (optional)

SERVES 6 TO 8 (2$^1\!/_2$ CUPS)

Combine the spinach, artichokes, basil, mayonnaise, Romano cheese, garlic and pepper in a bowl, mixing well. Spread evenly in a 9-inch pie pan. Bake, covered, at 350 degrees for 25 minutes or until heated through. Do not overbake. Serve warm in a hollowed-out round loaf of bread.

LIGHT VERSION: Substitute light mayonnaise for regular mayonnaise.

ROASTED MEATBALLS IN BLUE CHEESE MADEIRA SAUCE

This is one of those versatile recipes where the sum is greater than its parts. The meatballs and sauce can be served separately in a variety of ways, but when joined together, they will transport you to heaven.

A.R.R. and L.A.R.

MEATBALLS

1 pound ground round
1/2 cup Italian bread crumbs
1/4 cup chopped onion
1 egg
2 tablespoons grated Parmesan or
    Romano cheese
1 tablespoon chopped fresh parsley
1 tablespoon chopped oregano
2 cloves of garlic, minced
1/8 teaspoon salt
1/8 teaspoon black pepper

BLUE CHEESE MADEIRA SAUCE

3/4 cup madeira wine
1 tablespoon minced shallots
1 cup heavy cream
1/4 cup unsalted butter, softened
3 ounces blue cheese, crumbled
1 tablespoon Dijon mustard
1/8 teaspoon white pepper
Pinch of nutmeg

MAKES 24 MEATBALLS AND 1 1/2 CUPS SAUCE

MEATBALLS: Combine the ground round, bread crumbs, onion, egg, Parmesan cheese, parsley, oregano, garlic, salt and pepper in a bowl. Shape into 24 equal-sized meatballs. Place in a single layer on a baking sheet. Bake at 350 degrees for 15 to 18 minutes or until cooked through.

BLUE CHEESE MADEIRA SAUCE: Simmer the madeira and shallots in a large skillet until the shallots are golden and the madeira is almost evaporated. Stir in the cream. Simmer until the mixture is reduced to 3/4 cup. Mash the butter, blue cheese, mustard, white pepper and nutmeg in a small bowl. Whisk the blue cheese mixture into the cream sauce over low heat until thoroughly incorporated. Stir in the cooked meatballs. Cook over low heat until heated through.

NOTE: The sauce can be made ahead and refrigerated. Reheat by placing in the top of a double boiler over simmering water or in a skillet over low heat. Cook until heated through, stirring constantly.

VARIATION: Try this sauce over pasta with wild mushrooms or replace the meatballs with mushrooms for a vegetarian hors d'oeuvre.

BLACK BEAN SPIRALS WITH FRESH TOMATO SALSA

This is one of our most popular hors d'oeuvres. It is also a great dip! The rolls can be made a day ahead of time and then sliced and served right before guests arrive.

A.R.R. and L.A.R.

BLACK BEAN FILLING

1 cup cooked black beans

8 ounces cream cheese, softened

1 clove of garlic, chopped

$1/2$ teaspoon salt

$1/4$ teaspoon Jo B's Firemud or other hot pepper sauce

2 tablespoons diced red bell pepper

1 teaspoon chopped jalapeño pepper, seeded

FRESH TOMATO SALSA

1 pound ripe tomatoes (4 small tomatoes), cut into chunks

$1/4$ cup chopped onion

$1/4$ cup chopped green bell pepper

$1/2$ jalapeño pepper, seeded and diced (1 tablespoon)

2 sprigs cilantro, stems removed (2 tablespoons)

1 green onion, chopped

1 clove of garlic, chopped

ASSEMBLY

4 (8-inch) flour tortillas

MAKES ABOUT 48 SPIRALS

BLACK BEAN FILLING: Process the black beans and cream cheese in a food processor until well blended. Add the garlic, salt and hot pepper sauce. Process to blend. Pulse in the red pepper and jalapeño pepper. Refrigerate, covered, for 2 hours. Makes $1^3/4$ cups filling.

FRESH TOMATO SALSA: Pulse the tomatoes, onion, green pepper, jalapeño pepper and cilantro just until blended. Drain off any excess liquid and transfer to a bowl. Stir in the green onion and garlic. Refrigerate, covered, until ready to use.

ASSEMBLY: Lay the tortillas out in a row. Spread $1/2$ cup black bean filling evenly over the lower $3/4$ of each tortilla. Roll up each tortilla tightly toward the unspread edge. Wrap each tightly in plastic wrap. Refrigerate for 2 hours or until firm. Unwrap the tortillas. Slice both ends off of each tortilla and discard. Then slice each crosswise into 12 spirals. Arrange the spirals in a concentric pattern on a serving platter. Place a dollop of fresh tomato salsa on 1 side of each spiral.

Baked Brie in Puff Pastry with Dried Cherry Chutney

1 (17-ounce) package frozen puff
   pastry, thawed
1 (2-pound) Brie cheese wheel
   (10-inch diameter)
1 egg
1 tablespoon water
French bread slices
Jo Anna's Dried Cherry Chutney
   (page 83)

SERVES 20

This is an impressive hors d'oeuvre that takes very little time and is well worth the effort. In the summer it can be served with fresh nectarines and strawberries. In the fall, use ripe pears and apples. The chutney adds a special flavor that can be stuffed between the Brie layers or served alongside a piece of warm Brie and fresh bread.

A.R.R.

Place 1 sheet of the puff pastry on a lightly floured board. Roll into a 10-inch square. Place the Brie wheel in the center of the pastry square and cut around the wheel to exact diameter of Brie. Roll out the second puff pastry sheet and cut a 14-inch circle. Place Brie in center of 14-inch circle. Place smaller 10-inch circle over top of Brie. Mix egg and water in bowl. Brush egg wash over edges of 14-inch circle and fold over the top of Brie, sealing edges. Brush egg wash over entire top of pastry. Combine pastry scraps into a ball and roll out to ¼-inch thickness. Cut into shapes, such as stars or hearts, for decorations, using a cookie cutter. Brush the cutouts with the egg wash and attach to the seam around the top pastry circle. Place the Brie on an ungreased baking sheet. Bake at 400 degrees for 35 to 45 minutes or until the pastry is golden. Let stand at room temperature for 30 minutes before serving so the cheese isn't too soft and runny. Garnish with fresh fruit, kale and flowers. Serve with French bread and dried cherry chutney or summer fruit chutney.

NOTE: Occasionally the melted Brie will leak out of the pastry and run all over the baking sheet. If this happens, let the cheese cool, then scoop it up and place under the bottom of the wrapped Brie.

VARIATION: The Brie wheel may be cut in half horizontally and filled with dried cherry chutney or another chutney or Boursin Cheese (page 44). Reassemble the Brie after filling it and proceed as directed above.

JO ANNA'S DRIED CHERRY CHUTNEY

This recipe comes from an amazing chef friend, Jo Anna Jenkins. One day I asked Jo Anna to make a chutney from dried cherries and asked if she needed a recipe as a guideline. She whipped up this creation and wrote down the ingredients so that we could duplicate it. Don't be overwhelmed by the number of ingredients. It is relatively fast to make—about 1/2 hour once you have all the ingredients assembled.

A.R.R.

1 large sweet onion, minced

1/2 cup minced red bell pepper

1/2 cup minced yellow bell pepper

1 rib celery, minced

2 cups dried cherries

1/4 cup minced gingerroot

1 jalapeño pepper, minced

3 tablespoons minced shallots

2 cloves of garlic, minced

1/2 cup honey

1/2 cup red wine vinegar

1/3 cup packed brown sugar

1/4 cup port wine

2 tablespoons tarragon vinegar

1 tablespoon molasses

1 teaspoon chopped fresh tarragon
   leaves

1/2 teaspoon chipotle powder
   (optional)

1 cinnamon stick

MAKES 2 1/2 CUPS

Combine the cherries, onion, red pepper, yellow pepper, celery, gingerroot, jalapeño pepper, shallots, garlic, honey, red wine vinegar, brown sugar, wine, tarragon vinegar, molasses, tarragon, chipotle powder and cinnamon stick in a large heavy pot. Cook over medium-low heat for 1 hour, stirring frequently.

NOTE: Chutney can be stored in the refrigerator in an airtight container for up to 2 weeks.

SERVING SUGGESTION: This chutney is delicious with pork and poultry and can also be used to stuff a wheel of Brie cheese.

Why I Love Weddings

*I*n the catering business I have the opportunity to cook for many types of events and functions. Weddings give me the greatest satisfaction and joy. Having the opportunity to get to know two people who are planning such an important step in their lives and following the vision through to the day of their wedding is so special. I cherish being allowed to have a glimpse into their world. By the time the actual wedding day arrives, I feel like we are throwing a big party for friends. Weddings provide me with an opportunity to really go all out and create the most beautiful delicious food possible. I am always in awe at how magically the whole day comes together. I can only hope—as one mother wrote me—that their lives together can turn out to be as wonderful.

A.R.R.

American Flatbread

To have this recipe in our cookbook is an honor. To serve this bread at every event is a ritual. To know George Schenk and his staff and have them in our community is a blessing.

Most of the food that we provide through our Catering business is made from scratch in our kitchen. This is a very strong commitment to ourselves and our clients. We make one exception quite happily: American Flatbread.

American Flatbread was built with integrity. They produce a product that is created with only organic ingredients that are the finest available. From the water gathered directly from the stream above their property to the organic flour used to make the dough, flatbread will not compromise on ingredients or method for any reason.

Most of our staff at one time or another has worked with our friends at American Flatbread. When we serve George's breads, we top them with our own savory combinations of roasted peppers and goat cheese, capers, red onion and olives, or perhaps smoked shrimp and basil pesto.

We go to Flatbread on Friday nights to be nourished physically, emotionally, and spiritually. Fresh baked Flatbread from George's clay oven can't be described with words. Not only is our physical hunger satisfied but we are surrounded by friendly familiar faces, peace and prayer flags, and messages of hope in the form of weekly dedications on the menus. Enough good can't be said about how much George, Chris, Camilla, Paul, and the Flatbread Family means to us. Thank You.

Thank You...

For feeding not just our stomachs but our hearts and spirits as well,

For showing us the meaning of Integrity and Quality in both the materials that go into Flatbread as well as the people who make it.

For the words of wisdom both simple and profound that have been a part of each night's dedication that remind us of what is real and what is important,

For the thousands of Flatbreads that have been given to sick children and people in need. May your good will continue to heal.

Most of all, thanks for all the T.L.C. that you put into the food and serve the food with.

We are so blessed to have you in our community.

AMERICAN FLATBREAD

4 tablespoons cold spring water

$^1/_4$ ounce cake yeast, or

   2 tablespoons active dry yeast

2 pounds organic flour

1 teaspoon kosher salt

Olive oil

Fresh garlic

MAKES 2 FLATBREADS

Warm 1 tablespoon of the water and combine with yeast in a medium bowl. Let sit for 4 minutes. After the yeast has been activated, add the remaining 3 tablespoons water. Combine the flour and salt. Add to the yeast mixture, stirring until all the ingredients are well incorporated. Turn the dough onto a lightly floured surface. Cover and let rise until doubled. Punch down the dough and form into 2 (14- to 16-ounce) pieces. Shape each piece of dough into a disk. Let rise again. Prepare your favorite toppings. Spread each dough disk into a 12-inch circle. Brush with olive oil and top with garlic and additional toppings. Bake in your wood-fired, handmade clay oven!

NOTE: For conventional use, sprinkle cornmeal on lightly oiled pizza pan. Bake at 375 degrees for approximately 15 minutes.

Fabulous Antipasto Presentation

The photograph on the preceeding page brings to your eye one of our signature hors d'oeuvres. Following are some of the techniques and recipes that we use to create our display that, when combined on the large board, make up the whole. Because time is often a factor when preparing for guests at home, we have also included a list of items that can be purchased from the store that will cut down production time and allow more fun time for the presentation.

STORE BOUGHT LIST:
Smoked salmon
Smoked white fish
Goat cheese
Assorted olives
Sun-dried tomatoes packed in oil
Marinated artichokes
Marinated mushrooms
Meats such as prosciutto, capocollo

DECORATING IDEAS:
Use radicchio, fresh basil, rosemary and other fresh herbs, edible flowers, whole rose petals, red or yellow peppers that have been scooped out to hold dips and spreads.

GOAT CHEESE ENCASED IN EDIBLE FLOWERS AND HERBS

TECHNIQUES AND TIPS:
Remove the petals from calendula, colorful pansies, borage, or any other edible organically grown (pesticide-free) flowers. Remove the leaves from fresh herbs and the green tops from green onions. Make sure the petals, herbs, and onion tops are very dry. Finely chop into a colorful confetti. Sprinkle the flower and herb confetti over goat cheese to create a festive, colorful look.

ROASTED GARLIC

Cut $1/4$ of the top off 4 garlic heads to expose the cloves. Peel off any loose, dry skin. Place the garlic, cut sides up, in a baking dish. Add enough water to the dish to reach a depth of $1/4$ inch. Drizzle olive oil over the tops of the cloves. Cover the dish with foil. Bake at 450 degrees for about 45 minutes.

ROASTED PEPPERS

Rub the outside of the peppers with olive oil. Place on a baking sheet. Roast for about 40 minutes. Turn the peppers over. Roast for 15 minutes. Place in a bowl and cover with plastic wrap and let cool. Peel off the skin and remove stems and seeds. Cut into julienne strips.

EGGPLANT CAPONATA

$\mathcal{T}$his recipe is extremely versatile. It can be used as a dip, salsa, or sauce for pasta.

A.R.R.

2 pounds eggplant

6 tablespoons extra-virgin olive oil, divided

2 cups chopped sweet onion

1 cup chopped fennel or celery

1 cup chopped red bell pepper

1 teaspoon minced garlic

1 (28-ounce) can tomatoes

1/4 cup red wine vinegar

3 tablespoons sugar

1/2 teaspoon salt

1/4 teaspoon freshly ground pepper

1 cup golden raisins

1/4 cup drained capers

6 kalamata olives, pitted

1/4 cup pine nuts, toasted

1/2 cup chopped fresh basil leaves

SERVES 8 TO 10

Peel eggplant and cut into 1-inch cubes. Heat 4 tablespoons of the olive oil in a large skillet. Add the eggplant. Sauté for about 10 minutes or until golden brown. Remove to a bowl; set aside. Heat the remaining 2 tablespoons oil in the same skillet over medium heat. Add the onion, fennel and red pepper. Sauté for about 5 minutes or until tender. Stir in the garlic. Cook for 1 minute. Add the drained and chopped tomatoes, vinegar, sugar, salt and pepper. Bring to a boil; reduce the heat. Simmer, uncovered, for about 10 minutes, stirring frequently. Stir in the golden raisins, capers and olives. Simmer for 15 minutes or until the eggplant is tender. Remove from the heat. Taste and adjust the seasonings, adding additional sugar, vinegar, salt and pepper to achieve a good balance of sweet and acidic flavors. Cool to room temperature. Stir in the pine nuts and basil just before serving.

NOTE: Relish can be stored in the refrigerator in an airtight container for up to 1 week.

CARAMELIZED ONIONS

1/4 cup olive oil

8 cups thinly sliced onions

1 teaspoon salt

2 tablespoons balsamic vinegar

1 tablespoon brown sugar

MAKES 2 1/4 CUPS

Heat the olive oil in a large heavy skillet over medium-low heat. Add the onions and salt. Cook, covered, until the onions are golden, stirring occasionally. Uncover. Add the vinegar and brown sugar. Cook for 15 to 20 minutes or until all the liquid has evaporated. Increase the heat to medium. Cook until the onions are evenly browned, stirring often. Cool to room temperature.

MINIATURE CRAB CAKES WITH CHIPOTLE AIOLI SAUCE

These crab cakes are always a hit. This recipe was created for landlocked states, like Vermont, that don't have native crab. Feel free to use fewer bread crumbs as filler if you are one of those lucky locals who has access to fresh crab.

A.R.R.

CRAB CAKES

1 tablespoon each minced red and yellow bell pepper
1 tablespoon minced red onion
1 tablespoon butter
1 pound cleaned crab meat
1 cup plain bread crumbs
5 tablespoons mayonnaise
2 tablespoons Worcestershire sauce
1 tablespoon Dijon mustard
1 tablespoon chopped fresh parsley
1 tablespoon chopped fresh chives
1 teaspoon ground white pepper
Clarified butter (see Note)

CHIPOTLE AIOLI SAUCE

1 cup mayonnaise
1/2 cup caramelized onions (page 91)
1 tablespoon minced chipotle chiles in adobo sauce
2 teaspoons lime juice
1/2 cup roasted garlic purée
1/8 teaspoon salt
1/2 teaspoon black pepper

MAKES 55 (1-INCH) CRAB CAKES

CRAB CAKES: Cook the minced vegetables in 1 tablespoon butter over low heat until tender. Cool. Combine the crab meat, bread crumbs, vegetable mixture, mayonnaise, Worcestershire sauce, mustard, parsley, chives and white pepper in a bowl; mix gently. Shape the crab mixture into 1-inch patties about the size of a quarter. Heat the clarified butter in a large skillet over medium-high heat. Add the crab cakes and cook until lightly browned on both sides. Serve on heart-shape toasts with chipotle aioli sauce.

NOTE: This recipe for clarified butter may be used to make any quantity. Make only as much as you need for the recipe.

CLARIFIED BUTTER: Melt the butter in a saucepan over low heat. Transfer the melted butter to a bowl. Let cool. The clarified butter, or pure butterfat, will rise to the top. Skim off this clear yellow liquid and set aside for cooking. Discard the white solids and water that remain in the bowl.

CHIPOTLE AIOLI SAUCE: Combine the mayonnaise, caramelized onions, chiles in adobo sauce, lime juice, roasted garlic purée, salt and pepper in a bowl. Refrigerate, covered, until ready to use. Makes about 2 cups.

VARIATION: For Roasted Red Pepper Aioli Sauce, substitute 3/4 cup chopped roasted red bell pepper for the chipotle chiles.

LOBSTER-FILLED PHYLLO TRIANGLES SERVED WITH CORN RELISH

One evening while recipe testing for this book, I discovered that these triangles were better grilled on the barbecue than baked in the oven! I had intended to test how long it would take to bake these and instead put a few on the grill. I was so excited by my experiment that we changed the recipe! When making these in the summer, cook them on the grill. In the cooler months, bake them in the oven and fill the house with their aroma.

L.A.R.

¹/₄ cup cooking sherry

2 shallots, minced

4 sprigs fresh tarragon

³/₄ cup heavy cream

*³/₄ cup diced steamed lobster meat
    (1¹/₂ pounds lobster)*

¹/₄ cup fresh bread crumbs

2 teaspoons minced fresh tarragon

Salt and pepper to taste

2 (14x18-inch) sheets phyllo dough

Melted butter

*Sweet and Smoky Corn Relish
    (page 95)*

MAKES 12 TRIANGLES

Combine the sherry, shallots and tarragon sprigs in a saucepan. Cook over medium heat until the liquid is evaporated. Stir in the cream. Cook until the mixture is reduced by half. Strain into a bowl, discarding the tarragon sprigs. Add the lobster meat, bread crumbs, 2 teaspoons tarragon, salt and pepper. Mix gently to combine. Stack the 2 phyllo sheets. Cut with sharp kitchen scissors or a knife at 3-inch intervals along the 18-inch side of the sheets to form 6 strips. (There will be a total of 12 strips, each 3 inches wide and 14 inches long.) Cover the phyllo strips with a damp kitchen towel to prevent them from drying out. Work with 1 strip at a time, keeping the remaining covered. Lightly brush 1 strip of phyllo with butter.

To shape a triangle, place about ¹/₂ tablespoon of the lobster filling at the end of the strip nearest you. Fold the left-hand corner of the strip diagonally over the filling to form a triangle. Continue folding over at right angles, as you would fold a flag, to form a triangular-shaped package. Tuck the top edge into the nearest fold. Repeat with the remaining phyllo strips and lobster filling. (The triangles may be prepared ahead to this point. Refrigerate on a covered tray for several hours before baking.)

Spray a baking sheet with vegetable cooking spray. Arrange the phyllo triangles in a single layer on the baking sheet. Brush the tops of the triangles with melted butter. Bake at 350 degrees for 25 to 30 minutes or until golden brown. Transfer the triangles carefully to a serving platter. Place a small dab of sweet and smoky corn relish on each triangle.

SWEET AND SMOKY CORN RELISH

Kevin Dunn, one of our chefs, created this recipe and we all love it! This relish can also be served with fish or chicken.

A.R.R.

$^{1}/_{4}$ *cup rice vinegar*

2 tablespoons sugar

$^{1}/_{4}$ *cup finely diced zucchini*

$^{1}/_{4}$ *cup finely diced yellow squash*

$^{1}/_{4}$ *cup peeled, seeded and finely diced tomato*

$^{1}/_{4}$ *cup fresh or frozen corn kernels*

$^{1}/_{4}$ *cup finely diced red onion*

2 tablespoons reconstituted chopped sun-dried tomatoes

1 jalapeño pepper, seeded and finely chopped

2 tablespoons extra-virgin olive oil

1 teaspoon liquid smoke

$^{1}/_{4}$ *teaspoon salt*

MAKES 1 CUP

Combine the vinegar and sugar in a saucepan. Cook over medium-low heat until the sugar is dissolved. Stir in the zucchini, yellow squash, tomato, corn, red onion, sun-dried tomatoes, jalapeño pepper, olive oil, liquid smoke and salt. Cook for 4 minutes. Remove from the heat. Cool and set aside. Drain the excess liquid.

VEGETABLE FRITTERS WITH ROAST GARLIC PARMESAN DIP

These fritters are a beautiful golden brown studded with specks of autumn color. The vegetables can be anything that is readily available at the store or in your refrigerator. While the fritters are best served right out of the fry pan, they can be made an hour ahead and reheated in the oven.

A.R.R.

FRITTERS

1 (8-ounce) sweet potato

2 to 3 carrots

1¹/₃ cups zucchini

1¹/₃ cups yellow squash

1 finely chopped jalapeño pepper, seeds and stem removed

¹/₄ cup chopped green onion

¹/₄ cup flour

3 tablespoons fresh orange juice

1 tablespoon minced orange zest

2 tablespoons chopped fresh chives

1 tablespoon chopped onion

¹/₂ teaspoon salt

¹/₄ teaspoon pepper

1 egg white, beaten to stiff peaks

Vegetable oil for frying

DIP

²/₃ cup mayonnaise

¹/₃ cup sour cream

1 tablespoon garlic purée (page 90)

¹/₄ cup grated Parmesan cheese

1 tablespoon chopped fresh chives

2 teaspoons lemon juice

1 teaspoon hot pepper sauce

YIELDS 40 FRITTERS

FRITTERS: Peel and shred the sweet potato in a food processor. Peel and shred enough carrots in a food processor to measure 1¹/₃ cups. Remove seeds from unpeeled zucchini and yellow squash. Shred zucchini and squash in food processor. Combine the sweet potato, carrots, zucchini, yellow squash, jalapeño pepper, green onion, flour, orange juice, orange zest, chives, onion, salt and pepper in a medium bowl; mix thoroughly. Fold in the beaten egg white. Heat enough oil in a skillet to prevent the fritters from sticking. Drop 1 tablespoon of the vegetable mixture into the hot oil, being careful not to crowd the skillet. Fry for 3 to 5 minutes or until golden brown on all sides, turning if necessary. Drain on paper towels. Serve immediately with the roast garlic Parmesan dip.

NOTE: It is always best to cook one fritter first as a sample and adjust the seasoning to your taste. Add additional flour if fritters fall apart.

DIP: Whisk together the mayonnaise, sour cream, roasted garlic, Parmesan cheese, chives, lemon juice and hot pepper sauce in a bowl until well combined. Refrigerate, covered, until ready to serve. Thin with milk if necessary. Makes 1 cup.

ROASTED BUTTERNUT SQUASH AND APPLE SOUP

his is one of our most popular and requested soups. The flavor and colors are perfect for the autumn. With the addition of maple syrup and apple cider, it is a true Vermont classic! Serve with our ginger crème fraîche.

A.R.R.

SOUP
3 pounds butternut squash
2 cups apple cider, divided
¼ cup unsalted butter
2 tart apples (about 2¼ cups),
  peeled and chopped
1 cup sliced leeks (white part only)
⅓ cup chopped onion
1½ cups chopped celery
¼ cup maple syrup
1 teaspoon cinnamon
¼ teaspoon freshly ground nutmeg
5 cups water
½ to 1 cup milk or half-and-half
  (optional)
Salt to taste

GINGER CRÈME FRAÎCHE
1 cup heavy cream
½ cup sour cream
1 teaspoon grated gingerroot, or
  ½ teaspoon ground ginger

GARNISH
Freshly ground nutmeg
Crystallized ginger

SERVES 10

SOUP: Peel the butternut squash and cut in half. Remove and discard the membranes and seeds. Place the squash halves in a large baking pan. Add 1 cup of the apple cider. Cover the pan with foil. Bake at 400 degrees for 30 minutes. Remove the foil. Bake until the squash is completely soft; set aside.

Melt the butter in a Dutch oven. Add the apples, leeks, onion and celery. Sauté until the onion begins to turn transparent. Stir in the cooked squash, maple syrup, cinnamon and ¼ teaspoon nutmeg. Cook over low heat for 3 to 5 minutes or until heated through. Add the water and remaining cup apple cider. Bring to a simmer. Remove from the heat. Purée the soup in a blender or food processor until smooth, adding desired amount of milk or cider for a smoother texture. Season to taste with salt and additional maple syrup and cinnamon.

GINGER CRÈME FRAÎCHE: Whisk the heavy cream and sour cream together in a mixing bowl. Cover the bowl with plastic wrap. Let sit at room temperature for 8 hours or until the mixture is thick. Line a strainer with cheesecloth or a paper coffee filter. Set the strainer over a bowl. Pour the thickened cream mixture into the lined strainer. Cover with plastic wrap. Refrigerate overnight to let the cream drain into the bowl. Stir the gingerroot into the thickened cream. Store in a covered glass jar in the refrigerator for up to 1 week.

GARNISH: Top each serving of soup with a dollop of Ginger Crème Fraîche, a sprinkle of nutmeg and a piece of crystallized ginger.

WILD RICE PANCAKES

These pancakes make a wonderful side dish to a poultry main course. The first time I made these I ate six pancakes right off the griddle because they were so delicious!

A.R.R.

2 quarts water
3/4 cup uncooked wild rice, rinsed
    and drained (1 1/2 cups cooked)
1 large onion, finely diced
3 cloves of garlic, minced
2 teaspoons chopped mixed fresh
    herbs (oregano, sage, basil and
    thyme), or 1/2 teaspoon dried
    herbs
1/4 cup unsalted butter
8 ounces white button mushrooms,
    coarsely chopped
10 shiitake mushrooms, thinly
    sliced (5 ounces)
2 tablespoons olive oil
3 tablespoons soy sauce
1/4 cup minced fresh parsley
5 eggs, separated
1/2 to 3/4 cup flour
4 ounces shredded Cheddar cheese
4 ounces Parmesan cheese, grated
Vegetable oil for frying

MAKES 14 (3-INCH) PANCAKES

Bring the water to a boil in a saucepan. Stir in the wild rice. Return to a boil; reduce the heat. Simmer, covered, for 45 minutes to 1 hour or until the grains are tender and beginning to burst. (The rice should be tender, but slightly chewy.) Drain, return to the saucepan and set aside.

Sauté the onion, garlic and mixed herbs in the butter in a large skillet for 15 minutes or until the onion is tender. Add the onion mixture to the rice. Sauté the mushrooms in the olive oil in the same skillet until golden brown, stirring often. Add the mushrooms, soy sauce and parsley to the rice mixture and mix well.

Beat the egg yolks in a medium bowl until smooth. Add the egg yolks, 1/2 cup flour, Cheddar cheese and Parmesan cheese to the rice mixture and mix gently. Beat the egg whites in a large bowl until stiff, but not dry, peaks form. Fold the egg whites gently into the rice mixture.

Pour a thin film of vegetable oil into a large skillet. Heat over medium heat until hot. Spoon 2 tablespoons rice mixture for each pancake carefully into the hot oil, being careful not to overcrowd the skillet. Bake until golden brown on both sides. Transfer the cooked pancakes with a slotted spatula to paper towels to drain. Keep them warm in an oven set on a low heat setting until the remaining pancakes are cooked.

NOTE: It's a good idea to bake a test pancake to see if the seasoning is correct as well as to check for consistency. If the pancake is fragile and difficult to flip, stir up to 1/4 cup additional flour into the rice mixture.

Wild Rice Pancakes with Salmon Fillet in Puff Pastry

SALMON FILLET IN PUFF PASTRY WITH CITRUS BEURRE BLANC

This is definitely a special occasion dish. It can be made early in the day and then taken from the refrigerator to the oven. We always have a lot of fun in our kitchen cutting out the fish design and snipping scales with the scissors. Halibut, sea bass, or any other firm white fish can be substituted. This is not only easy, but impressive.

A.R.R.

SALMON

Juice of 1 lemon

2 teaspoons Worcestershire sauce

1 teaspoon salt

$1/2$ teaspoon pepper

4 (3-ounce) salmon fillets, skinned and boned

1 egg

1 teaspoon water

Pinch of salt

2 (17-ounce) packages frozen puff pastry, thawed

SALMON: Whisk together the lemon juice, Worcestershire sauce, 1 teaspoon salt and pepper in a bowl. Brush this mixture over the salmon fillets; set aside.

Make a cardboard cutout of a fish with a tail by referring to the picture on page 99. Make sure that your cutout is slightly larger than the salmon fillets so that it will completely encase the fillets, plus have a small border beyond them to allow you to seal the pastry.

Beat the egg, water and a pinch of salt in a bowl; set aside. Roll out each sheet of puff pastry, 1 at a time, on a lightly floured surface. Cut out a total of 8 pastry fish, 2 per sheet, by tracing around the cardboard fish with a sharp knife. Place the pastry fish in a single layer on a parchment-paper-lined baking sheet or a lightly sprayed sheet tray. Refrigerate the trays of fish as they are completed.

Work with 2 pastry fish at a time, keeping the remaining in the refrigerator. Lightly brush each pastry fish with the egg mixture. Place 1 salmon fillet on 1 of the pastry fish. Mold the salmon fillet to follow the shape of the pastry fish cutout. Brush the egg mixture lightly around the edges of the pastry. Cover the fillet with the second pastry fish, making sure the fillet is completely covered. Press the edges of the pastry together with fingertips, and then use the tines of a fork to make a tighter seal. Place on a parchment-lined baking sheet. (The recipe can be prepared several hours ahead to this point. Refrigerate, covered, until ready to bake.)

CITRUS BEURRE BLANC

1 cup dry white wine

Juice of ¹/₂ lemon (3 tablespoons)

1 shallot, minced (3 tablespoons)

¹/₄ cup heavy cream

1 cup chilled unsalted butter, cut into 16 chunks

Salt to taste

SERVES 6

Brush the egg mixture lightly over the entire fish. Repeat with the remaining pastry fish and salmon fillets.

Bake at 375 degrees for about 30 minutes or until golden brown. Serve with citrus beurre blanc.

NOTE: Before baking the fish, you can make them look more whimsical by making little snips with a sharp scissors over the bodies for scales and a few strokes with a paring knife on the tails. Also, a single caper can be inserted to simulate a fish eye.

CITRUS BEURRE BLANC: Combine the wine, lemon juice and shallot in a small saucepan. Simmer until the mixture is reduced to 1 tablespoon. Add the heavy cream and simmer until reduced by half. Remove from heat and add 1 piece of butter at a time while whisking constantly. You may need to return the saucepan to heat in order to incorporate all the butter. Be careful not to get sauce too hot or it will break. Strain sauce through a fine mesh sieve. Season with salt. Makes 1¹/₂ cups.

NOTE: This sauce can be made ahead and kept warm in a thermal container.

Designing Wedding Menus

A Traditional Buffet . . . The Modified Stations Concept . . . A Sit-Down Plated Meal . . . How Does One Choose?

One of the important decisions our catering clients make when planning their party is choosing a menu format for their meal. Some guests prefer the simplicity of a traditional buffet where the main entrées, side dishes, and salads are all on the same serving table and guests go through the buffet line and help themselves. Formal sit-down meals are truly elegant and offer a high level of guest service but limit the variety of foods that a guest is offered.

The newest concept in food formats is our favorite, the modified stations concept. Guests start the evening meal with a beautifully composed salad, wine service at the table, and an introduction about the evening from the waitstaff. The guests are invited to help themselves to one of at least two—but often many more—theme stations. Friendly chefs deliver piping hot pasta to order, carving chefs select the proper cut and doneness of meat to suit each individual's taste, and often dessert stations are the finale to the evening meal with pastries galore and, in Vermont, Ben and Jerry's Ice Cream Sundaes. We encourage clients to have fun with their menu planning and let the food experience be an active and memorable part of their event.

VERMONT TURKEY BREAST STUFFED WITH FRUITED CRANBERRY-SAGE DRESSING

Towards the end of August, we begin to see this dish appearing on our wedding menus and we know that summer is coming to an end in Vermont. Both staff and guests find comfort in this recipe, especially when served with mashed potatoes and cider gravy. Phil Kiendle, one of our chefs, created this delicious, moist cranberry jewel dressing that has a wonderful balance of sweet and tart.

A.R.R.

FRUITED CRANBERRY-SAGE DRESSING

2 cups diced peeled Granny Smith apples

1½ cups diced celery

1½ cups diced onions

½ cup diced dried apricots

½ cup dried cranberries

2 tablespoons vegetable oil

3 tablespoons finely chopped fresh sage leaves

2½ cups low-sodium chicken broth

½ cup butter

½ cup fresh cranberries

1 (14-ounce) package seasoned stuffing cubes

1 tablespoon poultry seasoning

1 tablespoon fresh thyme leaves

Salt and pepper to taste

1 (2-pound) boneless turkey breast half with skin

Salt and pepper to taste

FRUITED CRANBERRY-SAGE DRESSING: Sauté the apples, celery, onions, apricots and dried cranberries in the oil in a skillet for 2 minutes. Stir in the sage. Cook until the fruit and vegetables are tender; set aside. Bring the chicken broth to a boil in a large saucepan. Add the butter and cook until melted. Parboil the fresh cranberries in water to cover in a saucepan and drain. Place the stuffing cubes in a medium bowl. Add the broth mixture, fruit and vegetable mixture, parboiled cranberries, poultry seasoning, thyme, salt and pepper, mixing well; set aside. Makes 9 cups.

NOTE: May substitute 1 tablespoon dried sage for the fresh sage.

ASSEMBLY: Place the turkey, skin side down, on a cutting board. Cut a pocket in the breast with a sharp knife by slicing from the long, thin side towards the thicker side, being careful not to cut all the way through. Open the pocket and stuff with 2 cups of the cranberry-sage dressing. Pull the meat and skin back over the pocket. Truss with butcher's twine. (The remaining dressing can be spooned into a greased 2-quart baking dish and baked, covered, at 350 degrees for 30 minutes or until heated through.) Season the turkey with salt and pepper. Place in a roasting pan. Roast at 375 degrees for 1 hour or until a meat thermometer inserted in the turkey registers 165 degrees. Remove turkey from the pan. Cover and let stand for 10 minutes. Remove the twine from the turkey. Carve into ¾-inch slices.

APPLE CIDER GRAVY

2 cups unsalted turkey stock or
    low-sodium chicken broth
1/4 cup apple cider
1 tablespoon finely chopped shallots
1 1/2 tablespoons cornstarch
2 tablespoons water
Salt and pepper to taste

SERVES 4 TO 6

APPLE CIDER GRAVY: Pour off and discard the fat from the roasting pan, reserving the juices. Add the turkey stock, apple cider and shallots. Bring the mixture to a simmer, scraping the bottom of the pan with a wooden spoon. Cook slowly for 10 minutes. Make a paste of cornstarch and water. Pour the cornstarch mixture into the simmering broth, whisking constantly. Cook for 2 minutes. Season with salt and pepper to taste. Makes 2 cups.

NOTE: An average whole turkey breast weighs 5 to 6 pounds on the bone. Ask your butcher to take the breast off the bone, giving you approximately 2 (2-pound) breast halves. You may freeze one breast half for the future, or use both following the preceding directions, but doubling the gravy recipe.

CRANBERRY-GINGER COMPOTE

Juice and zest of 2 oranges
1 1/4 cups cider vinegar
1 cup packed brown sugar
1/2 cup maple syrup
1/2 cup golden raisins
1 onion, finely diced
1 tablespoon grated gingerroot
3/4 teaspoon salt
1/2 teaspoon allspice
1 1/2 pounds cranberries

MAKES ABOUT 4 CUPS

This compote is rich in color and taste. It goes well with turkey, duck, or poultry and will last for 2 to 3 weeks in the refrigerator if well covered.

A.R.R.

Combine the orange juice and zest, cider vinegar, brown sugar, maple syrup, golden raisins, onion, gingerroot, salt and allspice in a saucepan. Bring to a boil. Stir in the cranberries and cook for 15 minutes or until the mixture is thick. Remove from the heat and let cool.

GRILLED LOIN OF PORK SERVED WITH RED ONION CHUTNEY AND STEPHANIE'S SPICED APPLES

This is a wonderful dish that will guarantee great reviews. Stephanie's Spiced Apples on page 162 are not only a beautiful garnish but an incredible taste sensation with this pork.

A.R.R.

1 (3-pound) boneless pork loin
  roast, rolled and tied
6 tablespoons olive oil
2 tablespoons chopped garlic
1 tablespoon diced shallot
6 sprigs fresh thyme, stems removed
1 tablespoon salt
1 teaspoon black pepper
Red Onion Chutney (page 107)
Stephanie's Spiced Apples (page 162)

SERVES 8 (14 ONE-INCH SLICES)

Place the pork roast in a large sealable plastic food storage bag. Combine the olive oil, garlic, shallot, thyme, salt and pepper in a bowl. Pour over the pork. Press the air out of the bag and seal tightly. Marinate in the refrigerator for at least 1 hour or for up to 24 hours. Heat a gas grill to high. Grill the pork roast until seared and golden brown on all sides. Turn the grill temperature to low. Cook for 45 to 55 minutes or until a meat thermometer inserted in the roast registers 160 degrees, turning to cook evenly on all sides. Cover and let stand for 15 minutes before slicing. Serve with red onion chutney and Stephanie's spiced apples.

NOTE: To roast pork, heat 2 tablespoons vegetable oil in a large skillet over high heat until hot. Add the pork roast and brown on all sides. Transfer the pork to a roasting pan. Roast at 375 degrees for 1 1/4 hours or until a meat thermometer inserted in the roast registers 160 degrees.

VARIATION: Sprinkle dried herbs such as rosemary over the pork loin to give it a special look.

RED ONION CHUTNEY

This is one of the most versatile chutney recipes I've come across. It was adapted from the Country Garden cookbook series. We have added peaches, plums, nectarines, and pears and have come up with great combinations. The chutney can be made ahead and refrigerated, in a covered airtight container, for up to 2 weeks.

A.R.R.

1 tablespoon olive oil

3 medium red onions, finely chopped (3 cups)

1 jalapeño pepper, seeded and minced (1 tablespoon)

1 cup water

1 cup firmly packed brown sugar

3/4 cup red wine vinegar

1/2 cup golden raisins, chopped

1 Granny Smith apple, peeled and shredded

1/4 cup thinly sliced dry-packed sun-dried tomatoes

1 cinnamon stick

Salt to taste

MAKES 3 CUPS

Heat the olive oil in a large heavy saucepan over medium-low heat. Add the red onions and jalapeño pepper. Sauté for about 20 minutes or until the onions are tender. Stir in the water, brown sugar, vinegar, golden raisins, apple, sun-dried tomatoes and cinnamon stick. Simmer gently over low heat for about 1 hour or until all the ingredients are soft and the chutney begins to thicken, stirring frequently. (If the liquid has evaporated but the ingredients are not yet fully cooked, stir in some additional water.) Continue cooking until the chutney is reduced to a thick, jamlike consistency. Remove from the heat. Season with salt. Refrigerate, covered, for up to 2 weeks.

ORIENTAL VEGETABLE NOODLE SALAD WITH SESAME DRESSING

This noodle salad has become a trademark dish for Cooking from the Heart Catering. It has been served to the band Little Feat, Willie Nelson, many of Ben & Jerry's Homemade Ice Cream Company's employees, at the Mad River Music Festival, and to countless wedding guests. We always get the same response: "Can we have the recipe?" Well, here it is!

A.R.R.

16 ounces dried linguini

²/₃ cup soy sauce

¹/₄ cup sesame oil

¹/₄ cup red wine vinegar

¹/₂ cup chopped green onions

1 small jalapeño pepper, seeded and
    finely diced

3 tablespoons minced gingerroot

2 tablespoons minced garlic

2 tablespoons sugar or honey

1 cup julienned carrots, lightly
    blanched

1 red bell pepper, julienned

1 yellow bell pepper, julienned

1 small yellow squash, julienned

1 cup sugar snap peas (6 ounces)

¹/₂ cup sesame seeds, toasted

GARNISH

4 green onions, diagonally sliced

1 cup broccoli florets, lightly
    blanched

Additional toasted sesame seeds

SERVES 10 TO 12 (3¹/₂ QUARTS)

Cook the linguini in boiling water until al dente or tender, but firm. Drain and place in a serving bowl. Combine the soy sauce, sesame oil, vinegar, chopped green onions, jalapeño pepper, gingerroot, garlic and sugar in a bowl. Pour the dressing over the warm noodles and toss to combine. Add the carrots, red pepper, yellow pepper, yellow squash, peas and sesame seeds. Toss until combined.

GARNISH: Top with green onions, broccoli florets and sesame seeds.

VARIATIONS: Add grilled chicken slices, sautéed shrimp or tofu for a main course. May add ¹/₄ cup chopped cilantro to the salad.

EXOTIC SPINACH SALAD

This salad has a wonderful combination of sweet and tart flavors. The caramelized onions, mandarin oranges, red pepper, and shiitake mushrooms add color and depth. The dressing recipe comes from Heart n Hand in Virginia.

A.R.R.

1 small roasted red pepper
   (page 90)
10 ounces fresh spinach leaves
1 (11-ounce) can mandarin
   oranges, drained (¹/₂ cup)
1 cup Caramelized Onions (page
   91), or ¹/₂ cup sliced red onion
4 ounces shiitake mushrooms, sliced

SERVES 4 TO 6

Cut the pepper into strips. Clean and stem the spinach. Place the spinach leaves, mandarin oranges, caramelized onions, shiitake mushrooms and roasted red pepper strips in a salad bowl. Top with the desired amount of Creamy Citrus Dressing and toss gently until combined.

VARIATION: This salad is also great with maple balsamic dressing (page 129).

CREAMY CITRUS DRESSING

2 lemons
1 orange
¹/₂ cup sugar
1¹/₂ teaspoons fresh cracked pepper
1 teaspoon salt
2 cloves of garlic
2 cups extra-virgin or blended
   olive oil
1 cup fresh lemon juice
   (approximately 5 lemons)

MAKES ABOUT 4 CUPS

Wash the lemons and orange. Cut into quarters. Remove and discard all the seeds. Process the lemons, orange, sugar, pepper, salt and garlic in a food processor until very fine. Add the olive oil and lemon juice. Process to combine. Season to taste with additional salt, pepper and sugar. (This dressing will thicken. Thin with orange juice, if needed.)

GARLIC MASHED POTATOES WITH PARSNIP PURÉE

The addition of the parsnip adds a perfect touch of sweetness to these mashed potatoes. When I eat these, I just want to close my eyes and make time stop.

A.R.R.

1 pound parsnips, peeled (2 cups)

1/4 cup heavy cream

3/4 cup butter, softened and divided

2 teaspoons salt

1/2 teaspoon white pepper

4 large russet or Idaho potatoes (about 2 pounds), peeled and diced

2/3 cup hot milk or half-and-half

1/4 cup Roasted Garlic purée (page 90)

SERVES 6

Remove and discard the dense cores from the parsnips. Cut into 1/2-inch cubes. Cook in boiling water for 15 minutes or until tender. Drain and set aside.

Heat the cream in a saucepan or microwave in a microwave-safe bowl until hot. Process the parsnips, hot cream and 1/4 cup butter in a food processor until puréed. Season with the salt and pepper; set aside.

Cook the potatoes in boiling salted water until tender. Drain, shaking to remove any excess water. Return the potatoes to the saucepan. Cook over medium heat for 1 minute to evaporate any remaining moisture, stirring constantly. Mash quickly with an electric or hand mixer. Add the hot milk and remaining 1/2 cup butter slowly, mixing to combine. Stir in the parsnips and roasted garlic purée. Do not overmix.

"To cook well one must love and respect food."
—*Craig Claiborne*

NEW ENGLAND CORN PUDDING

This is my favorite corn pudding recipe. It is actually a cross between corn bread and spoon bread. It is total comfort food.

A.R.R.

7 cups fresh corn kernels
$^{1}/_{2}$ cup milk
$^{3}/_{4}$ cup butter, softened
6 tablespoons sugar
5 eggs, separated
5 tablespoons flour
1 tablespoon baking powder
1 teaspoon salt
1 cup shredded Cheddar cheese
1 cup diced red and green
    bell peppers

SERVES 16

Process the corn and milk in a food processor until puréed; set aside. Cream the butter with the sugar in a large bowl; set aside. Beat the egg yolks and add to the corn. Pour the corn mixture into the butter mixture and mix together. Stir in the flour, baking powder, salt, cheese and peppers. Beat the egg whites in a bowl until soft, firm peaks form. Fold the egg whites into the corn mixture gently. Pour into a greased 11x14-inch baking dish. Bake at 350 degrees for 45 minutes to 1 hour or until golden brown and a wooden pick inserted in the pudding comes out clean.

NOTE: To add spicy heat to the corn pudding, substitute some jalapeño peppers for the bell peppers.

"If the purpose of flavor is to arouse a special kind of emotion . . . that flavor must emerge from genuine feelings about the materials you are handling. What you are, you cook."
—*Marcella Hazen*

RAVIOLI WITH ROASTED BUTTERNUT SQUASH IN SAGE PASTA

This is one of our most requested ravioli recipes for modified buffets where Pasta Bar chefs serve hot cooked pasta to order. The filling is just sweet enough to make it different but has enough savory flavor to balance the taste. This can also be made with won ton wrappers if you choose. Try this with Sage Brown Butter Sauce (page 114) or Citrus Cream Sauce (page 116).

A.R.R.

SAGE PASTA
4 cups flour

2 teaspoons finely chopped sage leaves (veins removed from leaves)

6 eggs, beaten

BUTTERNUT SQUASH FILLING
2 cups roasted butternut squash (page 97)

1/4 cup grated Parmesan cheese (preferably imported)

1 egg yolk

5 tablespoons Vermont maple syrup

3/4 teaspoon freshly grated nutmeg

1/2 teaspoon salt

1/4 teaspoon pepper

ASSEMBLY
4 quarts water

1 tablespoon salt

SERVES 6 (MAKES 40 RAVIOLI)

SAGE PASTA: Process the flour and sage until the sage is evenly distributed in the flour. Add the eggs. Process until the dough comes together in a ball. (If the dough looks like small pebbles, add 1/2 teaspoon water at a time until a ball forms. If it is too wet, add 1 tablespoon flour at a time.) Remove the dough to a dry surface. Knead for about 2 minutes or until smooth. Wrap the dough in plastic wrap. Refrigerate for 1 hour.

BUTTERNUT SQUASH FILLING: Combine the butternut squash, Parmesan cheese, egg yolk, maple syrup, nutmeg, salt and pepper in a bowl; set aside. (Filling can be made ahead of time, covered and refrigerated.) Makes 2 1/4 cups.

ASSEMBLY: Divide the pasta dough into quarters. Work with 1 quarter at a time, keeping the remaining dough covered with plastic wrap. Flatten the dough portion into a disk. Run through the rollers of a pasta machine set at the widest position. Fold the ends of the dough towards the center and press down to seal. Run the open end of the dough through the widest setting again. Fold, seal and roll again. Without folding, run the dough through the widest setting 2 more times or until the dough is smooth. Continue running the dough through the machine, narrowing the setting each time. Dust the dough surface with flour if it becomes sticky. When finished rolling, the pasta sheet should be shiny and thin enough to see the outline of your hand through it. Cut the sheet into two 4-inch-long rectangles. Place about 1 tablespoon portions of butternut squash filling down the length of the pasta sheet, starting about 1 inch from the edge and leaving $1^{1}/_{4}$ to $1^{1}/_{2}$ inches between each portion of filling. Fold the other half of the pasta sheet over the filling to align with the opposite edge. Press the edges together to seal. Cut along the sealed edge and 2 sides of the pasta with a fluted pastry wheel. Cut between the filling with the wheel to form square ravioli. Repeat with the remaining pasta dough and filling. Bring 4 quarts water with 1 tablespoon salt to a boil in a large pot. Add half the ravioli. Return the water to a boil. Cook for about 5 minutes or until the edges are al dente. Transfer to a warmed bowl with a slotted spoon. Cook the remaining ravioli. Serve with your choice of sauce.

VARIATION:

WON TON RAVIOLI: This is the easy method for those who have not yet found a pasta godmother to apprentice with. Omit the pasta ingredients and substitute 80 won ton wrappers (2 packages).

For each ravioli, place 1 won ton wrapper on a lightly floured surface. Mound 1 tablespoon butternut squash filling in the center of the wrapper. Brush the edges of the wrapper with water. Place a second wrapper over the first. Seal the edges well, pressing to force out any air. Trim the edges with a fluted pastry wheel. Repeat until all the filling is used. Cook the ravioli, $^{1}/_{2}$ at a time, in a large pot of boiling salted water for 2 to 3 minutes or until they rise to the top and are tender. It is important not to let the water boil too vigorously or the ravioli may fall apart. Serve as above.

ROASTED GARLIC CREAM SAUCE

This sauce makes anything taste good! The reduction of wine and cream intensifies the flavors. While I don't recommend making this part of your weekly repertoire, it is definitely worth bringing out for special occasions.

A.R.R.

1/2 cup dry white wine

1 tablespoon chopped garlic

1 tablespoon chopped shallot

1 quart heavy cream

1/4 cup dry sherry

1 1/2 heads Roasted Garlic (page 90), puréed

Freshly grated nutmeg to taste

1/4 teaspoon salt

1/4 teaspoon pepper

MAKES 1 1/2 QUARTS

Combine the wine, chopped garlic and shallot in a saucepan. Cook over medium heat until reduced to 2 tablespoons. Stir in the cream. Cook until the sauce is reduced to 2 1/2 cups. (Watch carefully as the sauce scorches easily.) Stir in the sherry. Simmer for 10 to 15 minutes. Stir in the puréed roasted garlic. Strain sauce through a fine meshed sieve. Season with nutmeg, salt and pepper. Serve immediately.

SAGE BROWN BUTTER SAUCE

This was created to go with the Ravioli with Roasted Butternut Squash in Sage Pasta (page 112). The delicate nutty taste really complements the ravioli.

A.R.R.

1 cup unsalted butter

4 fresh sage leaves, chopped

MAKES 1/2 CUP

Heat the butter in a saucepan over medium-high heat for 4 to 5 minutes or until it begins to foam. Stir the butter constantly until it starts to brown. Remove from the heat. Stir in the chopped sage leaves.

TOMATO-BASIL MARINARA

This is one of our guests' favorite sauces at our Pasta Bar. Many people judge the food by how good the marinara tastes. This recipe has been handed down from Denise Fuoco's Nana. It's absolutely delicious!

L.A.R.

6 tablespoons extra-virgin olive oil
1/4 cup chopped cloves of garlic
4 (28-ounce) cans organic whole
   peeled tomatoes, chopped
   (12 cups)
1 bunch fresh basil leaves, chopped
   (1 cup)
Salt and pepper to taste

MAKES 11 QUARTS

Heat the olive oil in a large saucepan. Add the garlic. Sauté until a light golden color. Stir in the undrained tomatoes and basil. Bring to a boil; reduce the heat. Simmer, uncovered, for about 45 minutes or until thickened. Season with salt and pepper.

NOTE: This is also delicious as a pizza sauce.

SOUTHWEST PESTO

This recipe was created out of sheer imagination for a bride who requested a pesto with a southwestern flair. It is now a standard pesto that we offer to all of our clients.

L.A.R.

1 cup cooked black beans
1/4 cup chopped onion
1/4 cup fresh cilantro leaves
1 chipotle chile in adobo sauce
3 cloves of garlic
1 tablespoon red wine
1/4 teaspoon salt
1/4 cup olive oil

MAKES ABOUT 1 1/2 CUPS

Blend the black beans, onion, cilantro, chipotle chile, garlic, wine and salt in a blender or food processor. Add the olive oil in a slow stream with the machine running until almost smooth.

CITRUS CREAM SAUCE

Our chef, Sue Shickler, first made this dish for one of our smaller private parties. We were so impressed by the refreshing flavors of the citrus and cream combination that we added it to our Pasta Bar selection. People have gone wild for it ever since.

L.A.R.

3/4 cup dry white wine
1 tablespoon chopped shallot
1 quart heavy cream
1 lemon
3 tablespoons dry sherry
1 tablespoon sherry vinegar
1 tablespoon cornstarch (optional)
1 tablespoon water (optional)
Fresh grated nutmeg to taste
Salt and pepper to taste

Combine the wine and shallot in a saucepan. Cook over medium heat until reduced to 2 tablespoons. Stir in the cream. Cook until reduced by half. (Watch carefully as the sauce scorches easily.) Grate the zest and squeeze the juice from the lemon. Strain the juice to remove the seeds. Stir the zest and juice into the sauce. Add the sherry and sherry vinegar. Simmer for 15 minutes. The sauce should be thick and easily coat the back of a spoon. Adjust thickness, if necessary, with cornstarch mixed with water. Add to the sauce and cook for 1 minute. Season with nutmeg, salt and pepper. Serve immediately.

MAKES 1 QUART

TOMATO VODKA CREAM SAUCE

My sister Christy made this sauce for me quite a few years ago. It has become a Rossetto family favorite.

L.A.R.

1 1/2 cups finely chopped onions
2 tablespoons butter
1 (16-ounce) can organic whole
   peeled tomatoes, chopped
1 pint heavy cream
1/2 cup vodka
Pinch of crushed red pepper
1 cup grated Parmesan cheese

Sauté the onions in the butter in a skillet until tender. Add the undrained tomatoes. Simmer over low heat for 8 minutes. Stir in the cream. Simmer until reduced by 1 cup. Add the vodka. Simmer for 5 minutes. Stir in the red pepper. Simmer for 5 to 10 minutes or until the sauce reaches the desired consistency. Stir in the Parmesan cheese just before serving.

MAKES 5 CUPS

TUSCAN AL FRESCA SAUCE

This sauce, served at room temperature, is perfect in the summer as a dressing for a pasta salad. It is very flavorful and, if possible, should be made ahead at least 6 hours or overnight.

A.R.R.

1 pound vine-ripe tomatoes, seeded
    and chopped
1 medium onion, coarsely chopped
6 green olives, pitted and coarsely
    chopped
6 kalamata olives, pitted and
    coarsely chopped
2 cloves of garlic, minced
1/3 cup finely chopped fresh parsley
3 tablespoons chopped fresh basil
    leaves, or 1 teaspoon dried basil
1 tablespoon drained capers
1/2 teaspoon paprika
1/4 teaspoon dried oregano
1 tablespoon red wine vinegar
1/2 cup extra-virgin olive oil
Salt and freshly ground pepper
    to taste

MAKES 3 CUPS

Combine the tomatoes, onion, olives, garlic, parsley, basil, capers, paprika and oregano in a bowl. Drizzle with the vinegar and olive oil. Season to taste with salt and pepper. Marinate, covered, in the refrigerator for 6 hours or overnight. Serve at room temperature over hot pasta or use as a dressing for pasta salad.

Holiday Food &
Special Occasions

Rit.u.al (rich' oo-el) n. A procedure repeated customarily or automatically.

*W*hat would life be like without rituals? Luckily, I've never had to experience the answer to this question. When I was growing up, my mother and father owned a retail family floral business. Family is the operative word in that sentence. We lived together and worked together. But somehow, my mother always kept the element of surprise alive at holiday time. At our house, Santa brought the Christmas tree on Christmas Eve after we were all tucked in bed. Now that I have two children of my own, and work full time running a family business, I can't imagine how the five Simko children ever made it to the top of Santa's list to get not only heartfelt gifts, but a beautiful, fully decorated Christmas Tree. Sustaining traditions and upholding rituals is a priority in both Annie's life and mine.

The following recipes are our holiday favorites. We never need to be asked twice to cater a winter holiday party. The Strawberry Tree has shown up at my daughter's preschool for snack time and my mother Doreen can not attend a yearly holiday dessert party without bringing some variation of my Simple but Sinful Holiday Trifle.

A.M.D.

A SPECIAL HOLIDAY BUFFET

Brie Cheese with Warm Caramel Sauce

*Chutney-Glazed Cheese Pâté with Toasted Almonds
in a Festive Pine Cone Shape*

*Trio of Pancakes • Spinach Pancakes with Roasted Red Pepper
and Feta Cheese • Potato Latkes with Sour Cream and Apple
Compote • Carrot Pancake with Ginger Créme Fraîche*

*Beef Tenderloin Stuffed with Spinach, Basil
and Roasted Red Peppers • Horseradish Chantilly Cream*

Grilled Salmon Stuffed with Fresh Herbs and Citrus

Cucumber Dill Red Pepper Relish

Caramelized Onion and Fennel Gratin

Roasted Garlic Potato Fans

Roasted Winter Vegetables with Fresh Rosemary

*Boston Salad with Pears, Blue Cheese
and Toasted Walnuts • Maple Balsamic Dressing*

*Holiday Trifle with Eggnog Pound Cake, White Chocolate Custard,
Fresh Fruit and Frosted Cranberries*

Chocolate Chocolate Chip Brownie Trees with Peppermint Sticks

Festive Chocolate Dipped Strawberry Tree

BRIE CHEESE WITH WARM CARAMEL

BRIE CHEESE

    1 (2-pound) Brie wheel

    1 apple, sliced

    1 ripe pear, sliced

CARAMEL SAUCE

    ³/4 cup sugar

    ¹/4 cup water

    ¹/2 cup heavy cream

SERVES 15

This is a simple recipe that gets great results. The combination of cheese, apple, and caramel is sin-sational!

                    A.R.R.

BRIE CHEESE: Place the Brie in a pie plate or baking dish. Bake at 350 degrees for 15 minutes or just until the cheese is heated through and feels soft. Transfer the cheese to a festive holiday plate. Pour the caramel sauce over the Brie. Arrange the apple and pear slices around the Brie. Serve with assorted crackers or French bread.

CARAMEL SAUCE: Combine the sugar and water in a heavy saucepan. Cook over low heat until the sugar is dissolved, stirring constantly. Increase the heat to high. Cook until the mixture turns a golden caramel color. Remove from the heat. Whisk in the cream slowly and carefully, a little at a time. Serve warm or reheat over a double boiler.

CHUTNEY-GLAZED CHEESE PÂTÉ

    8 ounces cream cheese, softened

    1 cup shredded sharp Cheddar cheese

    3 tablespoons dry sherry

    1 teaspoon curry powder

    ¹/4 teaspoon salt

    ¹/4 cup mango chutney

    1 cup toasted whole unblanched almonds

SERVES 12

This is a great holiday appetizer that can be made up to two days in advance. It has a festive look as well as a great flavor.

                    A.R.R.

Process the cream cheese, Cheddar cheese, sherry, curry powder and salt in a food processor until smooth. Transfer the cheese mixture to a bowl. Refrigerate, covered, until firm. Shape the chilled cheese mixture with your hands into an oval that is tapered at one end. Spread the chutney over the surface. Press the rounded ends of the almonds into the cheese at a slight angle, starting at the tapered end and going towards the rounded end. Fill in all the empty spaces so the cheese with the nuts resembles a pine cone. Serve with assorted crackers.

TRIO OF PANCAKES

The following pancake recipes are dedicated to Joyce, my dear friend, who first introduced them to me during Chanukah. I have wonderful memories of standing in the kitchen and eating them right out of the fry pan as she made them.

A.R.R.

SPINACH PANCAKES WITH ROASTED RED PEPPER AND FETA CHEESE

*1 small onion, peeled and
  cut in half ($^1/_2$ cup)*
*4 cups fresh spinach leaves, or
  1 (10-ounce) package frozen
  spinach, cooked and drained*
3 eggs
$^1/_2$ cup matzo meal or flour
$^1/_4$ teaspoon nutmeg
$^1/_8$ teaspoon pepper
$^1/_2$ teaspoon baking powder
$1^1/_4$ teaspoons salt
Vegetable oil for frying
*Roasted red bell pepper strips
  (page 90)*
Feta or goat cheese, crumbled

**MAKES 2 DOZEN
MINIATURE PANCAKES**

Process the onion in a food processor until chopped. Scrape down the sides of the work bowl. Add the spinach and eggs. Process until mixed. Add the matzo meal, nutmeg, pepper, baking powder and salt. Pulse to combine. Heat enough oil in a large skillet to reach a $^1/_8$-inch depth. Drop the spinach mixture by tablespoonfuls into the hot oil, forming silver-dollar-size pancakes. Bake until golden brown on both sides. Remove from the skillet. Drain on paper towels. Top with strips of roasted red pepper and a sprinkle of feta cheese.

*"As our bodies are sustained with this food . . . May our hearts
be nourished with true friendship and our souls fed with truth."*

POTATO LATKES WITH SOUR CREAM AND APPLE COMPOTE

4¹/₂ cups grated peeled potatoes
1 onion, peeled and cut in quarters
2 eggs
¹/₂ cup matzo meal or flour
1 teaspoon baking powder
2 teaspoons salt
¹/₄ teaspoon pepper
Vegetable oil for frying
Sour cream

MAKES 3 DOZEN PANCAKES

CARROT PANCAKE WITH GINGER CRÈME FRAÎCHE

2 cups grated, peeled carrots
¹/₂ cup chopped green onions
3 eggs
¹/₂ cup flour
³/₄ teaspoon salt
¹/₂ teaspoon baking powder
¹/₈ teaspoon pepper
Vegetable oil for frying

MAKES 2 DOZEN MINIATURE PANCAKES

Process ¹/₂ of the potatoes and onion in a food processor until coarsely chopped. Add the eggs. Process until puréed. Add the remaining potatoes, matzo meal, baking powder, salt and pepper. Pulse to combine. Heat enough oil in a large skillet to reach a ¹/₂-inch depth. Drop the potato mixture by heaping tablespoonfuls into the hot oil, forming pancakes. Bake until golden brown on both sides. Remove from the skillet. Drain on paper towels. Serve topped with sour cream and applesauce or Apple Compote (page 62).

NOTE: It's a good idea to bake a test pancake to see if the seasoning is correct as well as to check for consistency. If the potato mixture is too runny, stir in more matzo meal or flour.

Process the carrots and green onions in a food processor until finely chopped. Add the eggs, flour, salt, baking powder and pepper. Pulse to combine. Heat enough oil in a large skillet to reach a ¹/₈-inch depth. Drop the carrot mixture by tablespoonfuls into the hot oil, forming silver-dollar-size pancakes. Bake until golden brown on both sides. Remove from the skillet. Drain on paper towels. Serve topped with small dollops of Ginger Crème Fraîche (page 97).

BEEF TENDERLOIN STUFFED WITH SPINACH AND BASIL

This is a great holiday recipe because of the red and green filling. In the summer, it is wonderful served at room temperature with our Horseradish Chantilly Cream.

A.R.R.

¹/₂ cup loosely packed basil leaves, thinly sliced

3 cups loosely packed chopped fresh spinach leaves

3 tablespoons butter

1 cup crumbled goat cheese or feta cheese

¹/₂ cup roasted red pepper

1 teaspoon chopped rehydrated sun-dried toamtoes

1 (2-pound) beef tenderloin

Salt and pepper to taste

1 tablespoon vegetable oil

HORSERADISH CHANTILLY CREAM

¹/₂ cup whipped cream

2 tablespoons crème fraîche

2 tablespoons prepared horseradish

Worcestershire sauce to taste

Tabasco sauce to taste

Pinch of salt

MAKES 10 (³/₄-INCH) SLICES

FILLING: Sauté the basil and spinach in butter and a splash of water for 1 minute or until bright green. Remove from heat. Add goat cheese, peeled roasted red pepper and sun-dried tomatoes.

BEEF TENDERLOIN: Trim any fat from tenderloin. Insert a clean knife-sharpening steel or other thick, pointed tool lengthwise through the center of the tenderloin. Rotate the tool to create a ¹/₂-inch-wide hole. Fill the hole in the center of the tenderloin with the spinach mixture, using the tool to push the filling toward the center from each end. Season the outside of the tenderloin with salt and pepper. Heat the oil in a large heavy skillet over high heat until hot. Add the tenderloin. Sear for 4 to 6 minutes or until browned on all sides. Transfer the tenderloin to a roasting pan. Roast at 350 degrees for 40 minutes or until a meat thermometer inserted in the meat registers 130 degrees for medium-rare. Let stand, covered, for 20 minutes before slicing.

HORSERADISH CHANTILLY CREAM: Combine the whipped cream, crème fraîche, horseradish, Worcestershire sauce, Tabasco sauce and salt in a bowl. Sour cream may also be substituted for crème fraîche.

GRILLED SALMON STUFFED WITH FRESH HERBS AND CITRUS

This is a spectacular presentation for a buffet that can be garnished to reflect the season. In the summer we use colorful edible flowers, lemon slices, and dill to decorate the salmon, and in the winter we use mâche, watercress, and red roses. The salmon can be served warm or at room temperature.

A.R.R.

1 bunch fresh basil
1 bunch flat-leaf parsley
2 bunches fresh dill
1 (4- to 6-pound) whole pan-dressed salmon (butterflied, with scales, head, tail and bones removed)
Salt and pepper to taste
8 lemons, peeled, seeded
Vegetable oil
Thinly sliced cucumber

CUCUMBER, DILL, RED PEPPER RELISH

¹/₂ cup rice wine vinegar
¹/₂ cup sugar
1 English or regular cucumber, peeled, seeded and coarsely chopped (1 cup)
¹/₂ cup coarsely chopped red bell pepper
¹/₂ cup diced yellow bell pepper
¹/₄ cup coarsely chopped red onion
¹/₄ cup chopped fresh dill, divided

SERVES 8 TO 10

GRILLED SALMON: Wash and dry the basil, parsley and dill. Remove and discard the stems. Open the salmon. Season the inside with salt and pepper. Layer the herbs and thinly sliced lemon on the salmon as follows: dill against the salmon flesh, then basil, parsley and lemon slices. Fold the salmon together. Rub the outside of the salmon with oil. Wrap tightly in heavy-duty foil. Grill the salmon over hot coals for 15 to 20 minutes on each side. Unwrap the salmon. Remove the skin carefully. Transfer the fish to a large platter. Slice into 8 to 10 pieces 1 inch in size, keeping the fish intact. Cover with thin slices of cucumber or cucumber, dill, red pepper relish.

NOTE: Ask your fishmonger to remove the scales, head, tail and bones from the salmon. The salmon can also be roasted in a 350-degree oven for 15 to 20 minutes per side.

CUCUMBER, DILL, RED PEPPER RELISH: Combine the vinegar and sugar in a small saucepan, stirring until the sugar dissolves. Simmer for 3 minutes. Remove from the heat and cool slightly. Refrigerate, covered, until chilled. Combine the cucumber, red pepper, yellow pepper, red onion and half the dill in a bowl. Pour the chilled vinegar mixture over the vegetables. Marinate, covered, in the refrigerator for at least 1 hour but for no more than 6 hours. Drain and stir in the remaining dill just before serving. Make 2 cups relish.

CARAMELIZED ONION AND FENNEL GRATIN

This recipe was created from pure desire. Leslie and I tasted this dish at the Bali Hai in Hawaii and knew we were going to have to duplicate it. This comes pretty close to the original. Have it in your oven baking when your guests arrive and they will go crazy!

A.R.R.

4 fennel bulbs
3 tablespoons butter, divided
2 tablespoons olive oil
2 large onions, thinly sliced (4 cups)
2 cloves of garlic, minced
Salt and pepper to taste
³/4 cup heavy cream
1 cup shredded Gruyère cheese
¹/2 cup fresh bread crumbs or
*   Japanese panko bread crumbs*

SERVES 6

Cut off the stalks from the fennel bulbs. Peel off the outer layer of each bulb and cut in half. Remove the cores if tough or stringy. Cut the bulbs into very thin slices. Steam the sliced fennel for about 20 minutes or until tender but firm; set aside. Melt 1 tablespoon butter with the olive oil in a large skillet. Add the onions. Cook, covered, over very low heat for 30 minutes or until golden brown and caramelized. Combine the onions, fennel and garlic in a bowl. Season with salt and pepper. Spoon into a buttered 9x13-inch baking dish or 3-quart shallow gratin dish. Heat the cream in a saucepan or microwave in a microwave-safe bowl until warm. Pour over the vegetables in the dish. Sprinkle with the Gruyère cheese. Melt the remaining 2 tablespoons butter in a skillet. Add the bread crumbs and toss to mix. Sprinkle over the cheese. Bake at 350 degrees for about 45 minutes or until brown and bubbly.

LIGHT VERSION: Omit the heavy cream and substitute the following béchamel sauce. Heat 1 tablespoon margarine or vegetable oil in a saucepan. Stir in 1 tablespoon flour. Cook for 1 minute. Stir 1 cup 2% milk in slowly. Cook for 3 to 5 minutes or until thickened, stirring constantly. Season with salt and pepper.

ROASTED GARLIC POTATO FANS

This is a beautiful roasted potato that looks special. The flavors are enhanced because the garlic and olive oil are able to penetrate during roasting, resulting in a delicious potato!

A.R.R.

6 medium potatoes,
    scrubbed and dried
3 cloves of garlic, thinly sliced
$1/2$ cup vegetable stock or low-
    sodium chicken broth
Olive oil
Salt and pepper to taste
Chopped fresh parsley

SERVES 6

Make a series of crosswise cuts, $1/2$ inch apart, across the width of each potato, forming slits. Cut only about halfway down through the potatoes, being careful not to cut all the way through. Insert the garlic slices into the slits. Place the potatoes in an oiled baking dish. Pour the vegetable stock over the potatoes. Drizzle with olive oil. Sprinkle with salt and pepper. Bake, covered, at 350 degrees for 30 minutes or until tender. Drain any liquid from the dish. Bake, uncovered, for 15 minutes or until the potatoes are golden brown. Arrange the potato fans on a serving platter. Sprinkle with chopped parsley.

NOTE: You may also rub the tops of the potatoes with chopped garlic for a real garlic lover's sensation. Garnish with sprigs of fresh thyme and rosemary.

ROASTED WINTER VEGETABLES WITH FRESH ROSEMARY

This combination of colors, flavors, and textures makes this dish a showpiece. It is a wonderful accompaniment to any entrée. I love to use leftovers as a base for roasted vegetable soups, or layered in lasagna with Roasted Garlic Cream Sauce (page 114) and fresh spinach. The vegetables can be interchanged depending on the season.

A.R.R.

1 pound butternut squash, peeled and cut into 1-inch cubes
1 pound parsnips, peeled and cut into 1-inch cubes
2 sweet potatoes, peeled and cut into 1-inch cubes
¹/₂ pound baby carrots, peeled
1 red bell pepper, cut into 1-inch slices
1 yellow bell pepper, cut into 1-inch slices
10 garlic cloves, peeled and left whole
Extra-virgin olive oil
Salt and pepper to taste
2 tablespoons chopped fresh rosemary leaves

SERVES 8

Place the butternut squash, parsnips, sweet potatoes and carrots on a large baking sheet. Place the red pepper, yellow pepper and garlic cloves on another baking sheet. Drizzle enough olive oil over the vegetables on each pan to lightly coat. Season with salt and pepper. Cover the baking sheets with foil. Bake at 400 degrees for 30 minutes. Uncover the vegetables and stir in the rosemary. Rotate the baking sheets to opposite oven racks to insure even roasting. Bake, uncovered, until the vegetables are golden and tender. (The vegetables will finish cooking at different times. Remove each type from the oven as it is done.)

Place the roasted vegetables in a large bowl. Toss together with salt and pepper to taste. Cover and keep warm until ready to serve. Place on a serving platter and garnish with sprigs of fresh rosemary.

Boston Salad

BOSTON SALAD WITH PEARS, BLUE CHEESE AND TOASTED WALNUTS

This is our favorite autumn salad. The textures and flavors work great together and our famous Maple Balsamic Vinaigrette is the perfect match.

A.R.R.

1 head Boston lettuce, separated
    into whole leaves
1 small head radicchio, separated
    into whole leaves
1 pear
Lemon juice
2 cups baby greens
3 ounces blue cheese, crumbled
1 cup walnut halves, toasted
1 head Belgian endive, separated
    into whole leaves

BOSTON SALAD: Arrange the largest Boston lettuce leaves around the edge of a shallow serving bowl or platter. Arrange most of the radicchio leaves inside the Boston lettuce leaves, forming a border. Cut the pear into slices. Brush the pear slices with lemon juice to prevent browning. Combine the pear, baby greens, remaining Boston and radicchio leaves, blue cheese and walnuts in a bowl. Add $^{1}/_{2}$ to $^{3}/_{4}$ cup maple balsamic vinaigrette to the baby greens mixture and toss to lightly coat. Arrange the baby greens mixture inside the lettuce/radicchio border in the serving bowl. Tuck the Belgian endive leaves under the salad so that the points are evenly spaced around the edge.

MAPLE BALSAMIC VINAIGRETTE

$^{1}/_{2}$ cup Vermont maple syrup
$^{1}/_{4}$ cup red wine vinegar
$^{1}/_{4}$ cup balsamic vinegar
$^{1}/_{4}$ cup tamari or light soy sauce
1 tablespoon minced shallots
2 teaspoons minced garlic
1 tablespoon Dijon mustard
2 cups extra-virgin olive oil
Salt and pepper to taste

VARIATION: An apple can be substituted for the pear and pecans for the walnuts. Dried cranberries can be added for color. The blue cheese can also be served on the side, as well as the dressing if serving this salad for a buffet.

MAPLE BALSAMIC VINAIGRETTE: Process the maple syrup, red wine vinegar, balsamic vinegar and soy sauce in a food processor until combined. Add the shallots, garlic and mustard. With the machine running, slowly add the oil. Process until emulsified. Season with salt and pepper.

SERVES 4

HOLIDAY TRIFLE WITH WHITE CHOCOLATE CUSTARD AND FROSTED CRANBERRIES

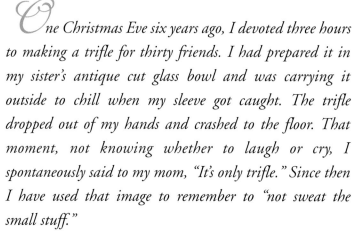

One Christmas Eve six years ago, I devoted three hours to making a trifle for thirty friends. I had prepared it in my sister's antique cut glass bowl and was carrying it outside to chill when my sleeve got caught. The trifle dropped out of my hands and crashed to the floor. That moment, not knowing whether to laugh or cry, I spontaneously said to my mom, "It's only trifle." Since then I have used that image to remember to "not sweat the small stuff."

A.R.R.

EGGNOG POUND CAKE

1/2 cup butter, softened

1 cup granulated sugar

2 eggs, beaten (room temperature)

1 cup eggnog

1 1/2 teaspoons rum extract

1 teaspoon vanilla extract

2 1/4 cups flour

2 teaspoons baking powder

1/2 teaspoon salt

3/4 teaspoon fresh grated nutmeg

BERRY SAUCE

2 cups fresh or frozen mixed berries (strawberries, blueberries, raspberries)

3 tablespoons granulated sugar, or to taste

2 tablespoons raspberry liqueur

EGGNOG POUND CAKE: Beat the butter and sugar with an electric mixer in a bowl until light and fluffy. Add the eggs gradually, beating until incorporated. Beat in the eggnog, rum extract and vanilla. Combine the flour, baking powder, salt and nutmeg in a bowl. Add to the eggnog mixture, mixing just until moistened. Pour the batter into a greased 5x9-inch loaf pan, spreading evenly. Bake at 350 degrees for 45 minutes or until a wooden pick inserted in the center comes out clean. Cool the cake in the pan for 10 minutes before removing from the pan to a wire rack. Cool completely.

BERRY SAUCE: Combine the berries and sugar in a medium saucepan. Bring to a boil; reduce the heat. Simmer for 3 to 4 minutes. Taste the mixture and add more sugar, if desired. Purée the berry mixture in a blender or food processor. Pour through a strainer into a bowl to remove the seeds. Stir in the raspberry liqueur. Refrigerate, covered, until chilled. (Sauce can be stored in the refrigerator for up to 2 days. It also freezes well.) Makes 1 1/2 cups.

WHITE CHOCOLATE CUSTARD

1/3 cup granulated sugar

2 tablespoons cornstarch

1/8 teaspoon salt

3 egg yolks

1 1/4 cups milk

1/2 teaspoon vanilla extract

1/2 teaspoon unflavored gelatin

1 tablespoon hot water

2 ounces white chocolate,
finely chopped

1/2 cup plus 2 tablespoons
heavy cream

FROSTED CRANBERRIES

1 egg white

Granulated sugar

Fresh cranberries

ASSEMBLY

4 cups assorted fresh fruit (sliced
strawberries, bananas, peaches,
raspberries)

1 pint heavy cream

3 tablespoons confectioners' sugar

1 teaspoon vanilla extract

SERVES 12

WHITE CHOCOLATE CUSTARD: Combine the sugar, cornstarch and salt in the top of a double boiler. Whisk in the egg yolks and milk until blended and smooth. Stir in the vanilla. Place over simmering water. Cook for 10 to 15 minutes or until the mixture thickens to a pudding consistency, stirring constantly. (Make sure to monitor the heat so the custard mixture does not get too hot and stir constantly to prevent a crust from forming.) Pour the custard into a bowl; set aside to cool. Combine the gelatin and hot water in a small bowl, stirring until the gelatin dissolves. Let stand for 5 minutes. Wash and thoroughly dry the double boiler top. Add the white chocolate and stir over hot water until melted. Mix the melted white chocolate into the gelatin mixture. Whip the heavy cream in a large bowl until soft peaks form. Fold a small amount of whipped cream into the white chocolate mixture. Add the white chocolate mixture to the remaining whipped cream and fold in gently. Fold a small amount of the whipped cream mixture into the cooled custard. Add the custard to the remaining whipped cream mixture and fold in gently; set aside. (Custard can be prepared ahead and stored, covered, in the refrigerator for up to 8 hours.) Makes 3 cups.

FROSTED CRANBERRIES: Beat the egg white in a small bowl until foamy. Pour some sugar into a small bowl. Brush each cranberry evenly with egg white, then roll in the sugar until evenly coated. Place on waxed paper and let stand for 1 hour or until dry. (These are used as a garnish, so make as many—or few—as you like.)

ASSEMBLY: Cut the pound cake into 1/4-inch slices. Line the bottom of a 3-quart trifle dish or straight-sided clear glass bowl with 1/3 of the cake slices, cutting them to fit snugly. Spread the cake with 1/3 of the berry sauce. Top with 1/3 of the assorted fruit. Spread 1/3 of the white chocolate custard over the fruit. Repeat the layers of cake, sauce, fruit and custard twice. Beat the heavy cream, sugar and vanilla in a bowl until soft peaks form. Top the trifle with whipped cream. Garnish with the frosted cranberries.

Chocolate Chip Brownie Trees with Peppermint Sticks

This is a great recipe for adults and children alike. I am always amazed at how quickly they disappear even at cocktail parties.

A.R.R.

10 tablespoons butter, melted and
    cooled

1¹/3 cups sugar

1¹/2 teaspoons vanilla extract

3 eggs, beaten

²/3 cup chocolate chips

²/3 cup flour

¹/2 cup baking cocoa (not Dutch
    processed)

¹/2 teaspoon baking powder

¹/2 teaspoon salt

Thin candy canes or peppermint
    sticks

MAKES 18 BROWNIE TREES

Combine the butter, sugar and vanilla in a mixing bowl. Beat the eggs in slowly. Stir in the chocolate chips. Combine the flour, cocoa, baking powder and salt in a bowl. Add the flour mixture to the butter mixture. Fold together gently just until barely mixed. Pour the batter into a greased 9x9-inch baking pan. Bake at 350 degrees for 25 to 30 minutes or just until the brownies begin to pull away from the sides of the pan. Remove from the oven and cool completely in the pan. Cut the brownies into nine 3-inch squares. Cut each square diagonally in half to form 18 triangles. Break the candy canes into small pieces and insert into the bottoms of the triangles for tree trunks.

DECORATING IDEA: Melt 2 ounces white chocolate in the top of a double boiler until smooth. (Or, place in a small microwave-safe bowl and microwave on High for 1 to 2 minutes, stirring halfway through the heating time.) Pour the melted white chocolate into a zipper-style plastic sandwich bag. Snip a tiny piece off 1 corner of the bag. Holding the top of the bag tightly with one hand and slowly applying pressure with the other, drizzle the chocolate in a zigzag fashion over the brownie trees to resemble garland.

FESTIVE CHOCOLATE-DIPPED STRAWBERRY TREE

My job at Cooking from the Heart is always one of varied tasks: from the front of the house, errand girl and copy diva to, of course, the kitchen. It came as no surprise when one wintry morning I was asked if I was feeling like arts and crafts—Annie-style. My mission was to make a chocolate-dipped strawberry tree for a holiday party. This is fun and easy to make.

L.B.M.

Semisweet chocolate

Fresh strawberries, hulls intact, rinsed and patted dry

Foam cone

Green, gold or red foil wrapping paper

Round wooden toothpicks

Fresh mint sprigs

Melt the chocolate in the top of a double boiler over simmering water until smooth. Dip each strawberry halfway into the melted chocolate. Place on a waxed-paper-lined tray. Refrigerate until the chocolate is set. Cover a foam cone with foil wrapping paper. Place the wide end of the cone into a serving bowl so that it fits snugly. The bowl prevents the tree from falling over. Insert toothpicks into the cone, about $3/4$ to 1 inch apart, forming a row near the bottom. Leave $1/2$ inch of each toothpick exposed. Press the stem ends of the dipped strawberries into the toothpicks. Repeat with additional toothpicks and remaining strawberries, adding 1 row at a time, until the cone is covered. Fill in any gaps with mint sprigs. Garnish the bottom of the tree with winter evergreens and pine cones.

NOTE: A 9-inch tree will use about 4 pints of strawberries. The finished tree can be prepared ahead and stored in a cool place until ready to serve. Do not refrigerate.

Aloha...A State of Mind

*S*omewhere in the throes of the 1997 summer catering season, Annie casually told me that she had been offered a job in Hawaii. Brugh Joy, famous author, workshop leader, and former client of Annie's, offered to fly her to his island retreat and have her cook for him for seven weeks. I didn't think the job offer was serious at first. When she brought it up a month later and gave me her departure date, I was in shock. I could not conceive how she was going to cover her business responsibilities, arrange child care for her thirteen-year-old son Ben, and basically step out of life as we know it for close to two months.

February of 1998 came quickly, and Annie was on a plane bound for Kauai. Priscilla, the new office manager of Cooking from the Heart Catering, and I were sitting in a room with more than 1500 cookbooks, a calendar overflowing with catering dates, and no Annie. Little did we know, Annie was beginning a journey that was about to change her life.

A.M.D.

One might be wondering why a chapter on Hawaii would be included in a cookbook centered around a Bed and Breakfast Inn in Vermont. Both of these places share an outward beauty that is breathtaking and something so special and magical that visitors immediately begin contemplating what it would be like to move there.

My seven-week stay on Kauai—the garden isle of Hawaii—was a journey that far exceeded the 4,956-mile, twenty-one-hour trip. The night before my departure, sitting in my office that looked like a bomb had exploded in it, I said to Anne Marie, "I feel so bad to be leaving you with all these loose ends but I really have to go . . . my soul needs to go." Looking at me and seeing into my heart as she always has, she said in her understanding and insightful way, "I know and it's O.K." With a big sigh of relief I began the incredible journey of discovering Aloha-State of Mind.

A.R.R.

ISLAND BREAKFAST

Banana Macadamia Nut Pancakes with Coconut Syrup

Pineapple-Stuffed French Toast

Island Banana-Coconut Bread with Rum Glaze

Tropical Coffee Cake

Iced Coconut Mousse with Tropical Fruit and Mango Sauce

AFTERNOON DELIGHTS

Chicken Satay with Peanut Coconut Sauce

Coconut Shrimp with Sweet and Spicy Pineapple Jalapeño Dip

Macadamia-Nut-Crusted Chicken Fingers

Papaya Chili Ketchup

Brugh's Island Joy Barbecue Sauce

Annie's Gratitude

It is with deep gratitude that I dedicate this chapter to three special people without whose support and assistance I could not have made this journey. First to Anne Marie DeFreest—the best friend a person could ever dream of and who I am convinced was sent to this earth as my guardian angel. It is because of her that my dream of writing a cookbook is now a reality. Next to Brugh Joy—a generous, caring man who believed in me enough to have me come cook for him and all the wonderful people who attended "Dream Time." And to Leslie Rossetto for making the time spent in the kitchen more fun than work and whose passion for life carries over in everything she does. Leslie took many of the recipes in this book and brought them to new heights.

I would also like to acknowledge all the wonderful people in Kauai—our visitors who gave so much—Mahola! Mariah, Kai, Mary, Pali, Chris, Mary Jo, Allen, Antoinette, Kathleen, Fishi, Lisabeth, James, Jacqueline, Connie, David D., Paula A.

A.R.R.

"It is the creative spirit—the inspiration and passion that comes through the person—that makes the food so wonderful."

BANANA MACADAMIA NUT PANCAKES WITH COCONUT SYRUP

These pancakes have a beautiful golden color and are absolutely delicious. The yogurt and banana purée make them moist and tender.

A.R.R.

PANCAKES

1¹/2 cups all-purpose flour

¹/2 cup whole wheat flour

2 tablespoons sugar

1 teaspoon salt

1 teaspoon cinnamon

2 cups plain or vanilla low-fat yogurt

4 eggs

1 cup puréed bananas (about 2 large bananas)

¹/4 cup butter, melted

2 teaspoons vanilla extract

2 bananas, coarsely chopped

COCONUT SYRUP

1 cup light corn syrup

¹/4 cup cream of coconut

GARNISH

¹/3 cup chopped macadamia nuts

1 cup sliced bananas

¹/2 cup toasted coconut

MAKES 16 (3-INCH) PANCAKES

PANCAKES: Combine the all-purpose flour, whole wheat flour, sugar, salt and cinnamon in a large bowl. Combine the yogurt, eggs, puréed bananas, melted butter and vanilla in a bowl. Add to the flour mixture. Stir just until moistened. Fold in the chopped bananas, being careful not to overmix. Spoon ¹/3 cup for each pancake onto a hot, greased griddle or skillet. Bake over medium heat for about 3 minutes on each side or until golden brown. Keep the pancakes warm (see Note). Serve warm with coconut syrup or hot Vermont maple syrup.

COCONUT SYRUP: Combine the corn syrup and cream of coconut in a saucepan. Simmer for 5 minutes, stirring constantly.

GARNISH: Sprinkle chopped macadamia nuts, bananas and toasted coconut over the pancakes.

NOTE: You can keep these pancakes warm until ready to serve by placing them on a platter or in a baking dish in a 200-degree oven. Layer paper towels between the pancakes to absorb steam and prevent them from getting soggy.

VARIATION: Blueberries, peaches or cooked apples can be substituted for the chopped bananas.

LIGHTER VERSION: Use egg substitute instead of eggs and reduce butter by half.

PINEAPPLE-STUFFED FRENCH TOAST

In Hawaii we had the good fortune of using a sweet Hawaiian bread that made the best French toast. Here in Vermont, challah, French, or Portuguese bread can also be used with equally good results.

A.R.R.

1 (12-inch) loaf Hawaiian sweet
    bread, challah, Portuguese sweet
    bread or French bread, unsliced
8 ounces cream cheese, softened
    (regular or low-fat)
2 cups drained canned crushed
    pineapple, divided
1/4 teaspoon cinnamon
6 eggs
1 cup heavy cream, half-and-half
    or milk
1 teaspoon nutmeg
1 teaspoon vanilla extract
4 tablespoons butter or vegetable oil

**MAKES 8 PIECES STUFFED
FRENCH TOAST**

Cut the bread into 16 (3/4-inch) slices. Beat the cream cheese, 1/2 cup crushed pineapple and cinnamon in a bowl until fluffy. Set aside. Beat the eggs, cream, nutmeg and vanilla in a bowl. Pour the egg mixture through a strainer into a 9x13-inch dish.

Add the remaining pineapple. Spoon 2 tablespoons cream cheese mixture onto 8 bread slices and cover with the remaining bread. Arrange the 8 French toast sandwiches in a single layer in the baking dish. Let stand until the bottom bread slices are completely moistened. Turn over and repeat on the other sides. Heat 2 tablespoons butter in a large skillet over medium-low heat. Add 4 sandwiches. Cook until golden brown on both sides. Repeat with the remaining 2 tablespoons butter and 4 sandwiches. Cut each French toast sandwich diagonally in half. Arrange on a serving platter and garnish with fresh mint and fresh fruit.

LIGHT VERSION: Substitute 1 1/2 cups egg substitute and 1 cup fat-free (skim) milk for the eggs and cream. Pour the milk mixture directly into the dish without straining it. Proceed as directed above.

ISLAND BANANA-COCONUT BREAD WITH RUM GLAZE

This recipe comes from the Caribbean via Vermont. The fresh ginger and lime make this banana bread stand apart from most other banana breads. Be prepared to give this recipe out.

A.R.R.

BREAD

3/4 cup packed brown sugar

1/2 cup butter, softened

1 cup mashed bananas (about 3 bananas)

2 eggs, lightly beaten

1/4 cup unsweetened coconut milk or yogurt

1 tablespoon fresh lime juice

2 cups flour

3/4 cup toasted flaked coconut

1 teaspoon baking powder

1 teaspoon grated gingerroot, or 1/2 teaspoon ground ginger

1/2 teaspoon salt

RUM GLAZE AND TOPPING

1/4 cup packed brown sugar

3 tablespoons fresh lime juice

1 tablespoon butter

1 tablespoon rum

1/3 cup toasted flaked coconut

MAKES 1 LOAF

BREAD: Cream the brown sugar and butter in a mixing bowl until light and fluffy. Add the bananas, eggs, coconut milk and lime juice. Beat until well blended. Combine the flour, toasted coconut, baking powder, gingerroot and salt in a bowl. Add the flour mixture to the banana mixture. Stir to combine. Pour the batter into a buttered 5x9-inch loaf pan. Bake at 350 degrees for 55 to 60 minutes or until a wooden pick inserted in the center comes out clean. Cool the bread in the pan for 10 minutes before removing from the pan to a wire rack. Cool completely.

RUM GLAZE AND TOPPING: Heat the brown sugar, lime juice, butter and rum in a small saucepan until the butter melts and the mixture thickens to a syrup consistency. Pour the glaze over the cooled loaf, spreading to coat the top and sides. Sprinkle the toasted coconut over the top.

TROPICAL COFFEE CAKE

The basis of this recipe comes from my friend, Kelly Wallace, whose parents have a restaurant called Tom's Riverside Grill in Bristol, Vermont. It is usually made with blueberries and is the best coffee cake I've ever eaten. In Hawaii, I adapted it using tropical fruits and toasted coconut. Leslie and I both agreed it was the best one yet!

A.R.R.

1 cup butter, softened

2 cups granulated sugar

2 eggs, room temperature

2 cups sour cream, room
   temperature

1 tablespoon vanilla extract

2 cups flour

1 tablespoon baking powder

1/4 teaspoon salt

1 cup toasted flaked coconut

2 1/2 cups chopped pecans

1/4 cup plus 2 tablespoons packed
   brown sugar

1 tablespoon plus 1 teaspoon
   cinnamon

1 cup chopped banana

1 cup chopped fresh pineapple

1 cup mango or papaya chunks

SERVES 12 TO 15

Beat the butter and granulated sugar in a mixer bowl until light and fluffy. Add the eggs, 1 at a time, beating well after each addition. Beat in the sour cream and vanilla until smooth. Combine the flour, baking powder, salt and coconut in a bowl. Fold the flour mixture into the sour cream mixture just until blended. Pour half the batter into a buttered 9x13-inch baking pan. Combine the pecans, brown sugar and cinnamon in a bowl. Arrange half the banana, pineapple and mango over the batter in the pan. Top with half the pecan mixture. Spoon the remaining batter into the pan, spreading evenly. Repeat layers of the remaining fruit and pecan mixture. Bake at 350 degrees for 1 hour or until a wooden pick inserted in the center comes out clean. Let the coffee cake cool for 30 minutes before serving.

NOTE: This coffee cake is best served the day it is baked. It can be frozen and reheated in a microwave oven.

VARIATION: Substitute 3 cups fresh or frozen blueberries, or 4 cups chopped peaches or apples, for the tropical fruits.

ICED COCONUT MOUSSE WITH TROPICAL FRUIT AND MANGO SAUCE

We made this dessert the last night of our eight-week stay in Hawaii. It was a big hit—cool, refreshing, a beautiful presentation with the fruit garnish. The best part was Lisabeth discovering that the leftover frozen mousse made the most incredible Piña Colada when adding fresh pineapple and rum!

A.R.R.

MOUSSE

- ⅔ cup shredded fresh coconut or flaked coconut
- ⅔ cup boiling water
- ⅔ cup unsweetened coconut milk
- 1 cup sifted confectioners' sugar, divided
- ¼ cup coconut cream or coconut liqueur, divided
- 2 tablespoons lime juice
- 1½ cups heavy cream, lightly whipped
- 4 egg whites
- ¼ teaspoon cream of tartar

MANGO SAUCE

- 1 cup water
- ½ cup granulated sugar
- 1 teaspoon lemon juice
- 2 mangos, peeled and pitted

SERVES 8 TO 10

MOUSSE: Combine the coconut, boiling water, coconut milk and 10 tablespoons confectioners' sugar in a small saucepan. Bring to a boil. Boil for 15 to 20 minutes or until the mixture has thickened, stirring frequently. Remove from the heat. Cool. Stir in the coconut cream and lime juice. Fold in the whipped cream. Beat the egg whites with the cream of tartar in a mixing bowl until stiff peaks form. Beat in the remaining 6 tablespoons confectioners' sugar, 1 tablespoon at time. Fold the egg white mixture gently into the coconut mixture. Do not overmix. Line a 4-cup mold or 5x9-inch loaf pan with plastic wrap. Spoon the coconut mousse into the prepared pan, spreading evenly. Cover with plastic wrap. Freeze for 4 to 6 hours or overnight. Unmold the mousse and slice. Serve with sliced fresh tropical fruits (mango, pineapple, papaya) and mango sauce.

MANGO SAUCE: Combine the water and sugar in a small saucepan. Cook over low heat until the sugar is dissolved, stirring constantly. Stir in the lemon juice. Bring to a boil. Remove from the heat. Cool and strain. Process the mangos in a blender or food processor until smooth. Strain and press through a sieve. Add the sugar syrup, 1 teaspoon at a time, until of the desired sweetness. Refrigerate, covered, until ready to serve.

Aloha is being a part of all
and all being a part of me.
When there is pain . . . it is my pain
When there is joy . . . it is mine also.
I respect all that is
as part of the Creator and part of me.
I will not willfully harm anyone or anything.
When food is needed I will take only my need
and explain why it is being taken.
The earth, the sky, the sea are mine
To care for, to cherish and to protect.
This is Hawaiian—This is Aloha."

Tales from the Night Rainbow
Pali Jae Lee, Koko Willis

CHICKEN SATAY WITH PEANUT COCONUT SAUCE

There are many chicken satay recipes, but this sauce/marinade is the most flavorful one I've eaten. When we were testing this recipe, I bypassed the chicken and began eating the sauce with a spoon. The sweet and hot are a perfect balance.

A.R.R.

8 (6-ounce) boneless skinless
  chicken breast halves
1 cup crunchy peanut butter
1/2 cup catsup
1/2 cup soy sauce
1/4 cup honey or packed brown
  sugar
1/4 cup lime juice
1/4 cup chopped cilantro leaves
  (optional)
1 bunch green onions, minced
6 cloves of garlic, minced
2 teaspoons salt
1/2 teaspoon cayenne
1/2 teaspoon black pepper
Coconut milk

MAKES 32 KABOBS

Soak 32 (8-inch) bamboo skewers in water for 1 hour. Cut each chicken breast half lengthwise into 4 strips. Combine the peanut butter, catsup, soy sauce, honey, lime juice, cilantro, green onions, garlic, salt, cayenne and black pepper in a bowl; blend well. Weave 1 chicken strip, accordion style, onto each bamboo skewer. Place the kabobs in a shallow glass dish. Reserve 1 cup of the peanut sauce. Pour the remaining sauce over the kabobs. Marinate in the refrigerator for several hours or overnight. Grill or broil the kabobs until the chicken is cooked through, turning halfway through the cooking time. Serve with the reserved peanut sauce for dipping, thinning it with coconut milk if necessary.

DECORATING IDEA: Place each skewer on an individual ti or lemon leaf and arrange on a flat basket tray or glass platter. Serve the sauce in a coconut shell or Asian bowl. Place an orchid or tropical flower on the corner of the tray near the sauce bowl.

VARIATION: The peanut sauce makes a wonderful dip on its own. Serve with cut-up fresh vegetables or thin with coconut milk and toss with cooked noodles.

COCONUT SHRIMP WITH PINEAPPLE JALAPEÑO DIP

This is a recipe that the staff never grows tired of, evidenced by the fact that there are never any leftover shrimp to eat, no matter how many extra we make.

A.R.R.

COCONUT SHRIMP

*1 pound large shrimp, peeled,
    deveined, washed and dried*
¹/₄ cup cornstarch
¹/₂ cup cream of coconut
2 tablespoons cornstarch
1 tablespoon lemon juice
1 teaspoon Worcestershire sauce
1 cup flaked coconut
*1 cup mild cracker crumbs or
    Japanese panko bread crumbs*
Vegetable oil for frying

PINEAPPLE JALAPEÑO DIP

*1 (20-ounce) can crushed
    pineapple, or 2 cups chopped
    fresh very ripe pineapple*
1 clove of garlic, peeled
2 tablespoons cream of coconut
1 tablespoon toasted flaked coconut
1 tablespoon heavy cream or milk
¹/₂ teaspoon salt
*2 jalapeño peppers, seeded and
    chopped*

MAKES 22 SHRIMP

COCONUT SHRIMP: Coat the shrimp with ¹/₄ cup cornstarch, shaking off any excess. Combine the cream of coconut, 2 tablespoons cornstarch, lemon juice and Worcestershire sauce in a bowl. Combine the flaked coconut and cracker crumbs in another bowl. Dip the shrimp in the cream of coconut mixture, shaking off any excess, then coat in the crumb mixture. Refrigerate the coated shrimp for at least 30 minutes. Pour enough oil into a large saucepan to reach a 3-inch depth. Heat the oil to 350 degrees. Drop the shrimp, 1 at a time, into the hot oil. Fry until golden brown. Serve with the pineapple jalapeño dip.

PINEAPPLE JALAPEÑO DIP: Process the undrained pineapple, garlic, cream of coconut, toasted coconut, cream and salt in a blender or food processor until smooth. Add a desired amount of jalapeño pepper. (The pepper will get hotter the longer the dip sits.)

SERVING IDEA: Arrange the shrimp on a platter or flat basket tray around a small bowl or ramekin with dip. Use pineapple leaves and fresh flowers, such as orchids, for decoration.

NOTE: The number of shrimp in a pouch will determine the number of pieces. This recipe used shrimp numbering 21 to 25 per pound.

MACADAMIA-NUT-CRUSTED CHICKEN FINGERS WITH PAPAYA CATSUP

This island version of chicken fingers will definitely stay in Vermont and be added to our repertoire. We could not stop eating them!

A.R.R.

CHICKEN FINGERS

8 boneless skinless chicken breast
    halves
1/2 cup soy sauce
1/4 cup sesame oil
1/2 cup chopped green onions
1 1/2 tablespoons red wine vinegar
1 1/2 tablespoons minced gingerroot
1 tablespoon sugar
1 tablespoon minced garlic
1 small jalapeño pepper, seeded and
    chopped
1 1/2 cups macadamia nuts or
    pecans, finely chopped
1 cup sweet bread crumbs or
    Japanese panko bread crumbs
1/2 cup flour
Salt and pepper to taste
4 eggs
1/4 cup vegetable oil
1/4 cup butter

PAPAYA CATSUP

1 papaya or mango, peeled, seeded
1/4 cup sweet chili sauce

SERVES 8

CHICKEN FINGERS: Pound each chicken breast for uniform width. Cut each chicken breast half into 4 to 6 strips, depending on size of chicken piece. Place in a large sealable plastic food storage bag. Combine the soy sauce, sesame oil, green onions, red wine vinegar, ginger, sugar, garlic and jalapeño pepper in a bowl. Pour over the chicken strips in the bag. Press the air out of the bag and seal tightly. Marinate in the refrigerator for 1 to 3 hours. Remove the chicken from the marinade; discard the marinade. Combine the macadamia nuts and bread crumbs in a shallow dish or pie plate. Season the flour with salt and pepper in another shallow dish. Lightly beat the eggs in a third shallow dish. Dredge the chicken strips in the seasoned flour, then dip into the eggs, shaking off the excess. Coat with the crumb mixture. Heat the oil and butter over medium heat in a large heavy skillet. Add the chicken strips, in batches if necessary. Sauté until golden brown on each side and cooked through, adding more oil to the skillet as needed. Keep warm until ready to serve. Serve with papaya catsup or Brugh's Island Joy Barbecue Sauce. Makes 32 chicken fingers.

PAPAYA CATSUP: Process the papaya in a blender until smooth. Strain through a mesh sieve. Add chili sauce and mix well. Makes 3/4 cup.

LIGHTER VERSION: Substitute 1 cup egg substitute for the eggs. Omit oil and butter. Spray the coated chicken strips with vegetable spray and place in a single layer on a baking sheet. Bake at 350 degrees for 10 minutes; turn. Bake for 10 minutes longer.

BRUGH'S ISLAND JOY BARBECUE SAUCE

This recipe is dedicated to Brugh, for all of his little-boy enthusiasm and appreciation of our island creations. Brugh really wanted to bottle this sauce so Annie and I could stay and live on Kauai. Thanks for everything, Brugh!

L.A.R. AND A.R.R.

1 cup minced onion

2 tablespoons vegetable oil

1 cup packed brown sugar

1 (8-ounce) can crushed pineapple

1 cup catsup

1 cup sambal olek (chili paste with garlic)

1 cup sweet chili sauce

1/2 cup pineapple juice

1/2 cup raspberry jam

1/2 cup apricot jam

1/2 cup red wine vinegar

2 tablespoons soy sauce

2 tablespoons Dijon mustard

MAKES 4 CUPS

Sauté the onion in the oil until transparent. Add the brown sugar and cook until dissolved. Combine the brown sugar and onion mixture with the undrained crushed pineapple, catsup, sambal olek, chili sauce, pineapple juice, raspberry jam, apricot jam, red wine vinegar, soy sauce and mustard in a medium saucepan. Bring to a boil; reduce the heat. Simmer, uncovered, for approximately 1 hour or until the sauce is thickened and coats the back of a spoon. Cool. Refrigerate, covered, until ready to use.

NOTE: Our favorite way to use this sauce is to pair it with baby back ribs, but it's also delicious on grilled chicken, the Macadamia Nut-Crusted Chicken Fingers on page 150 or Coconut Shrimp on page 149.

VARIATION: In Hawaii, 1 cup of Poha preserves can be used instead of the apricot and raspberry jam.

Top row standing, left to right: Kevin Dunn, Sue Shickler, Jim Gioia, Stephanie Koonz, Allison Duckworth, Robert Badore.
Middle row, left to right: Lisabeth Magoun, Kelly O'Hearn, Leslie Rossetto, Phil Kiendl, Annie Reed Rhoades, Doreen Simko, Jack Simko, Liz Van Hook, Kate Mahoney.
Front row, left to right: Denise Fuoco, Tiffany Benzing, Priscilla Vergura, Anne Marie DeFreest.

Our Staff's Favorites

*T*here is absolutely no connection or theme to the following recipes except the sheer and simple fact that they are from some of the most caring, creative, and concerned people that I have ever met.

Annie and I attribute a great deal of our success to the support we have received over the years from our staff. At the Round Barn, too many cooks don't spoil the pot . . . they enhance it.

In the fall, I eagerly await the first batch of Stephanie's spiced apples. She's been swapping pickle recipes with one particular guest for years. When Sue mentions that she might make her Pulled Pork and Coleslaw Sandwiches for staff lunch, our mouths start to water.

Please enjoy this eclectic collection of our Staff's Favorite Foods. We thank them all from the bottom of our hearts.

Annie and Anne Marie
Founders of A & A Enterprises,
Cooking from the Heart Catering
and The Inn at the Round Barn Farm

STAFF FAVORITES

Anne Marie's Comforting Beef Stew

Annie's Apple Pie with Cinnamon Crust

Almond Dream Cake with Fresh Strawberries and Whipped Cream

Oatmeal Soufflé

Leslie's Amazing Spiedini • Pasta Carbonara

Doreen's Mustard Sauce

Stephanie's Spiced Crab Apples

Louie's Baked Beans

Kate's Bailey's Irish Crème Chocolate Cheesecake

Denise's Biscotti • Lisabeth's Apricot Bars

Sue's Pulled Pork Barbecue Sandwich

Phil's Steak Salad with Grilled Vegetables and Feta Cheese

*Kevin's Portobello Mushrooms Stuffed
with Sun-Dried Tomato and Arugula Pesto*

Jim's Strawberry-Blueberry Pie

Kelly's Ginger Pear Cake

Mary's Vegetable Torta with Herbed Polenta Crust

Tiffany's Tuile Cigars with Raspberry Cream

Anne Marie's Comforting Beef Stew

3 tablespoons flour

1 teaspoon salt

1/2 teaspoon celery salt

1/2 teaspoon ginger

1/4 teaspoon garlic salt

1/4 teaspoon pepper

3 pounds beef stew meat, cut into
2-inch cubes

2 tablespoons vegetable oil

1 (16-ounce) can whole peeled
tomatoes

3 medium onions, sliced

1/2 cup molasses

1/2 cup water

1/3 cup red wine vinegar

6 to 8 carrots, peeled and cut into
1-inch pieces

1/2 cup raisins

SERVES 6 (YIELDS 7 CUPS)

Combine the flour, salt, celery salt, ginger, garlic salt and pepper in a large plastic food storage bag. Add the beef cubes, in batches, and shake a few times to evenly coat with the seasoned flour. Heat the oil in a large saucepan. Cook the beef in the hot oil until browned. Add the undrained tomatoes, onions, molasses, water and red wine vinegar. Bring to a boil; reduce the heat. Simmer, covered, over low heat for 2 hours, stirring in the carrots and raisins about 30 minutes before serving. At this point, I usually put a pot of water on to boil some wide egg noodles to serve along with the stew. If you prefer potatoes, you may add some to the stew with the carrots and raisins. Enjoy this wonderful winter comfort meal.

ANNIE'S APPLE PIE WITH CINNAMON CRUST

CINNAMON CRUST

2 cups flour
1/2 cup shortening
3 tablespoons butter
3 tablespoons sugar
1/2 teaspoon cinnamon
1/4 teaspoon nutmeg
Pinch of salt
6 tablespoons ice water

APPLE FILLING

7 cups sliced peeled apples
  (2 1/2 pounds)
3/4 cup sugar
2 tablespoons flour
1 tablespoon lemon juice
1 teaspoon cinnamon
1/2 teaspoon grated lemon zest
1/4 teaspoon salt
1/4 teaspoon nutmeg

ASSEMBLY

Cinnamon-sugar
3 tablespoons butter, cut into
  small pieces
Milk
Nutmeg

MAKES 1 (10-INCH) PIE

CINNAMON CRUST: Combine the flour, shortening, butter, sugar, cinnamon, nutmeg and salt in a food processor. Pulse just until the mixture has the consistency of cornmeal. Add the ice water. Pulse just until the dough comes together. Pinch a little of the dough between your fingers to test the consistency—it should feel like modeling clay, not too dry or sticky. Divide the dough in half and form into 2 flattened disks. Wrap in plastic wrap. Refrigerate for 30 minutes to 1 hour.

APPLE FILLING: Combine the apples, sugar, flour, lemon juice, cinnamon, lemon zest, salt and nutmeg in a bowl.

ASSEMBLY: Roll out half the pastry dough on a lightly floured surface to a 12-inch circle. Sprinkle both sides with cinnamon-sugar. Fit into a 10-inch pie pan. Spoon the apple filling into the crust. Dot the filling with the butter pieces. Roll out the remaining dough to a 12-inch circle. Place over the filling. Press the crusts together to seal and pinch to form a decorative edge. Brush the top crust with milk and sprinkle with cinnamon-sugar and nutmeg. Cut a few slits in the top crust with a sharp knife. Bake at 425 degrees for 30 minutes. Rotate the pie. Reduce the oven temperature to 375 degrees. Bake for 20 minutes or until the crust is golden brown and the filling is bubbling.

NOTE: With extra crust, design leaves to top the pie crust, using cookie cutters or cutting by hand. Secure into place with milk. A wonderful fall touch!

ALMOND DREAM CAKE WITH FRESH STRAWBERRIES

This cake has made me famous with my friends and family. The airy light cake, strawberries, and whipped cream are a perfect combination. I know some people who will buy this cookbook just for the recipe.

A.R.R.

CAKE

1 tablespoon melted unsalted butter

4 tablespoons amaretto, divided

2 teaspoons almond extract

4 eggs, beaten

3/4 cup sugar

1/2 cup roasted almonds

1/2 cup flour

WHIPPED CREAM FROSTING

3 cups heavy cream, chilled

1 tablespoon confectioners' sugar

1 1/2 teaspoons vanilla extract

ASSEMBLY

1 quart fresh strawberries

SERVES 8

CAKE: Combine the melted butter, 2 tablespoons amaretto and almond extract; set aside. Heat the eggs and sugar in a double boiler over hot water to about 100 degrees or just until warm. Remove the top of the double boiler. Whip the eggs with a handheld mixer for about 6 to 7 minutes or until they ribbon and peak; set aside. Pulverize the nuts in a food processor, adding the flour until fine. Fold the dry ingredients into the egg mixture 1/3 at a time, alternating with the amaretto mixture. Divide the batter evenly between 2 greased and floured 9-inch round cake pans. Place the pans in the center of the oven on separate racks. Bake at 375 degrees for 15 to 18 minutes or until a wooden pick inserted into the centers comes out clean. Cool in the pans for 10 minutes. Loosen the layers from the sides of the pans with a knife. Invert onto greased wire racks. Turn top sides up and immediately brush the layers with the remaining 2 tablespoons amaretto. Cool completely.

WHIPPED CREAM FROSTING: Pour the cream into a chilled bowl. Beat with chilled beaters at medium speed for 2 1/2 minutes or until thickened. Add the confectioners' sugar and vanilla, beating until stiff. Makes 4 cups.

ASSEMBLY: Slice all but 6 of the strawberries. Place 1 cake layer on a cake plate. Spread with a 1/2-inch-thick layer of whipped cream frosting. Top with the sliced strawberries. Place the second cake layer on top of the strawberries, pressing down to secure. Frost the top and side of the cake with the remaining frosting. Cut the remaining 6 strawberries in half, leaving the green stems intact. Arrange on top of the cake. Garnish with pansies, sliced almonds or fresh mint.

Oatmeal Soufflé

I consider this recipe the most brilliant recipe I have ever come across. It originally appeared in Marion Cunningham's *Breakfast Book,* my copy of which looks like the Velveteen Rabbit, for I have referred to it so many times that the cover is falling apart and the pages are well worn. Over the years I have adapted this recipe to make it lighter, added more spices for a different flavor, but the original recipe itself still remains a mystery to me. How can oatmeal, which is considered dense and heavy, be made into a soufflé? What would inspire someone to even attempt to create a recipe that seems like such an oxymoron, or contradiction in terms? I remember the first time I read this recipe . . . I remained skeptical all the way through until I read the very last line, "This soufflé is still tasty when cold and fallen!"

I have had a lot of fun with this recipe, knowing that each time I serve it someone will find their way into the kitchen and tell me how much they hate oatmeal but how much they loved the soufflé. I quietly say to myself, another oatmeal convert!

The Oatmeal Soufflé has become a metaphor for my life. Sometimes it works out, and sometimes it doesn't. Once one understands the mechanics of the soufflé the chance of its success is increased. However, by its very nature—as with life— there are unseen forces that may effect a negative outcome. It is at times like this that one is humbled, feels disappointment, and holds onto the memory of what is possible.

The Oatmeal Soufflé, as its name implies, holds all of life's contradictions: a fragile creature, yet remarkably strong. It can collapse with a breeze and is consumed in a few minutes. Is it worth all the commotion and the possible disappointment? The answer certainly is YES! For in that brief journey from oven to table lies our hopes, dreams, and excitement of creating a culinary delight that has challenged us and brought a smile to the recipient.

OATMEAL SOUFFLÉ

1 cup milk (2% or skim)

1 tablespoon butter

3/4 cup quick-cooking oats

1/3 cup light cream cheese

1/2 cup packed brown sugar or
    maple syrup

2 teaspoons cinnamon

2 teaspoons nutmeg

1/4 teaspoon salt

3 egg yolks, beaten, or 1/2 cup egg
    substitute

4 egg whites

SERVES 6

Heat the milk and butter in a heavy saucepan until the mixture is barely boiling. Stir in the oats. Cook over low heat for 1 minute or until the oats are cooked, stirring often. Remove from the heat. Add the cream cheese, brown sugar, cinnamon, nutmeg and salt. Stir until the cream cheese is completely melted and the mixture is well blended. Add the beaten egg yolks slowly to the oat mixture, stirring constantly. Beat the egg whites in a mixing bowl until stiff peaks form. Fold the egg whites gently into the oat mixture. Do not overmix. Spoon into a greased 2- to 3-quart soufflé dish or deep baking dish. Bake at 325 degrees for 45 minutes or until the center is firm when pressed. Serve immediately with milk, chopped nuts or Vermont maple syrup.

"To love what you do and feel that it matters—how could anything be more fun?"
—Katherine Grahm

LESLIE'S AMAZING SPIEDINI

This recipe was one of my father's favorites. He adapted it from Romeo Salta's Restaurant in Manhattan. Since I've been making it here in Vermont, my friends just won't let me stop. It is especially delicious for lunch.

L.A.R.

4 ounces high-quality anchovies
  with oil

2 tablespoons extra-virgin olive oil

⅓ cup chopped garlic

Juice of 2 lemons (¼ cup)

2 tablespoons capers, drained

4 ounces fresh mozzarella cheese,
  sliced ¼ inch thick

4 slices white bread

¼ cup unsalted butter

1 cup milk

1 cup flour

2 eggs, beaten

½ cup chopped fresh parsley

**MAKES 4 SERVINGS
(8 TRIANGLES)**

Heat the anchovies in a skillet until melted. Add the olive oil and garlic. Sauté for 4 minutes. Stir in the lemon juice and capers. Remove from the heat; set aside. Divide the mozzarella cheese slices between 2 bread slices. Top with the remaining bread slices to form 2 sandwiches. Cut each sandwich diagonally in half twice to form 4 triangles. Melt the butter in a large skillet. Dip the triangles in the milk, then in the flour and eggs. Cook in the melted butter until golden brown on both sides. Reheat the caper sauce if necessary. Place the triangles on a serving platter and pour the sauce on top of each. Sprinkle with the parsley.

PASTA CARBONARA

Many people think carbonara is a cream sauce served with prosciutto and peas. Not so. It is a delectable dish containing pancetta, onion, eggs, and cheese.

L.A.R.

8 ounces pancetta or slab bacon,
  cut into small cubes
1 medium onion, halved and sliced
3 eggs
¹/₂ cup chopped fresh parsley
¹/₂ cup grated Romano cheese
Salt and pepper to taste
1 pound linguini

SERVES 4 TO 6

Cook the pancetta in a skillet until the fat is rendered. Remove the pancetta with a slotted spoon to paper towels to drain; cool. Add the onion to the drippings in the skillet. Sauté until lightly browned. Beat the eggs in a medium bowl. Add the pancetta, onion, parsley, Romano cheese, salt and pepper; set aside. Cook the linguini until al dente or tender, yet firm. Drain. Immediately toss with the pancetta mixture. Garnish with additional parsley and cheese. Serve immediately.

DOREEN'S MUSTARD SAUCE

¹/₂ cup packed brown sugar
2 egg yolks
2 tablespoons dry mustard
1 tablespoon flour
¹/₂ teaspoon salt
1 (14-ounce) can sweetened
  condensed milk
¹/₂ cup vinegar

MAKES ABOUT 1¹/₂ CUPS

Combine the brown sugar, egg yolks, dry mustard, flour and salt in the top of a double boiler. Stir some of the condensed milk in gradually until smooth. Stir in the remaining condensed milk. Stir the vinegar in slowly. Cook over simmering water until the mixture is smooth, hot and thick enough to coat a spoon. Cool. The sauce will keep indefinitely if stored in a covered container in the refrigerator. Serve with baked smoked ham at a holiday gathering as I have for Simko family dinners.

STEPHANIE'S SPICED CRAB APPLES

Just when you think canning season is over, the crab apples are ripe and ready to be spiced. The easiest way to get the apples is to shake the tree branches and then pick the fallen apples off the ground. Be sure to leave the stems on the apples. Whenever you are canning, be sure you have enough time set aside so that you don't have to hurry. Check to make sure you have enough ingredients if you plan to make more than one batch. It's also a good idea to sterilize a couple of extra jars just in case you might need them.

3 pounds crab apples with stems
1¹/₂ tablespoons whole allspice
1¹/₂ tablespoons whole cloves
2 sticks cinnamon
6 cups sugar
3 cups water
3 cups cider vinegar

MAKES 4 QUARTS

Rinse the apples and prick each 3 or 4 times with a sterilized needle. This prevents the apples from bursting. Tie the allspice, cloves and cinnamon in a cheesecloth bag. Combine the sugar, water and vinegar in a large saucepan. Add the spice bag. Bring to a boil. Boil for 5 minutes. Add the apples to the pan in batches, 1 layer at a time, simmering each batch gently for 2 minutes or until tender. Remove the apples with a slotted spoon to a large bowl. Bring the pickling liquid to a boil. Remove from the heat. Ladle the liquid and spice bag over the apples. Cover. Let the apples stand for 12 to 18 hours in a cool place. (I put them in the cellar.) Remove the spice bag and apples from the liquid. Pour the liquid into a saucepan. Bring to a boil. Pack the apples into 4 hot, sterilized quart canning jars, leaving ¹/₄ inch headspace. Ladle the hot spiced liquid over the apples. Remove the air bubbles. Cover with 2-piece caps. Process the apples for 15 minutes in a boiling water canner.

Serve with ham, pork or roast beef. Makes a great gift for the holidays!

LOUIE'S BAKED BEANS

Louie is our very own Stephanie Koonz's husband. Stephanie treats the staff to Louie's baked beans whenever there are leftovers . . . which is not often!

1 pound dried navy beans, sorted and rinsed
8 cups cold water
¹/₄ pound bacon slices, cut into 1-inch pieces
1 cup beef bouillon
¹/₂ cup molasses
¹/₃ cup catsup
¹/₄ cup chopped onion
¹/₂ teaspoon dry mustard or curry powder (or both)
Additional bouillon

SERVES 10

Place the beans in a large saucepan. Cover with the water and let soak overnight. Bring the soaked beans to a boil; reduce the heat. Simmer for 30 minutes; drain. Place the beans in a greased 3-quart ovenproof bean pot or deep baking dish. Stir in the bacon, beef bouillon, molasses, catsup, onion and dry mustard. Bake, covered, at 250 degrees for 6 to 8 hours, uncovering the beans during the last hour of cooking. Add more bouillon during baking so that the beans are always covered with liquid. These beans are delicious served plain or with Vermont maple syrup!

KATE'S BAILEY'S IRISH CRÈME CHOCOLATE CHEESECAKE

CRUST

35 (about) chocolate wafer cookies

1/4 cup unsalted butter, melted

FILLING

3 (8-ounce) packages cream cheese, softened

3/4 cup granulated sugar

3 eggs

1/3 cup Bailey's Irish Crème liqueur

1 teaspoon vanilla extract

3 ounces imported white chocolate, finely chopped

TOPPING

1 1/2 cups sour cream

1/4 cup confectioners' sugar

1 1/2 ounces imported white chocolate, grated

1 ounce semisweet chocolate, grated

SERVES 10 TO 12

CRUST: Process enough chocolate wafer cookies in a blender or food processor to make 1 3/4 cups finely ground crumbs. Add the melted butter in a slow stream, processing until the mixture forms pea-size crumbs. Pat the crumb mixture over the bottom and 1 inch up the side of a 9-inch springform pan. Refrigerate for 30 minutes.

FILLING: Beat the cream cheese and sugar in a large bowl with an electric mixer until smooth. Whisk the eggs, liqueur and vanilla in a medium bowl just until blended. Beat into the cream cheese mixture. Add the finely chopped white chocolate, blending well. Pour the filling into the chocolate crumb crust. Bake at 325 degrees for 50 to 55 minutes or until the edges are puffed and the center is set. Cool completely on a wire rack.

TOPPING: Combine the sour cream and confectioners' sugar in a small bowl. Spread over the cooled cheesecake. Refrigerate for 6 hours or until well chilled. Sprinkle the grated white and semisweet chocolates over the top just before serving.

DENISE'S BISCOTTI

2¹/₂ cups flour

1¹/₄ cups sugar

1 teaspoon baking powder

1 tablespoon grated orange zest

¹/₂ teaspoon anise seeds

Pinch of salt

3 eggs

2 egg yolks

1 teaspoon vanilla extract

¹/₂ teaspoon anise extract

1¹/₂ cups whole almonds, toasted

MAKES 16 COOKIES

Combine the flour, sugar, baking powder, orange zest, anise seeds and salt in a bowl. Beat the eggs and egg yolks in a large bowl. Add the vanilla and anise extract. Stir the flour mixture gradually into the egg mixture. Mix until sticky, then stir in the almonds. Turn the dough onto a well-floured surface. Divide the dough in half with floured hands. Roll each half into a 12-inch log. Place the logs on a greased and floured baking sheet. Bake at 350 degrees for 25 to 30 minutes or until golden. Remove from the oven and let stand until cool enough to handle. Reduce the oven temperature to 275 degrees. Slice the logs crosswise on an angle into ¹/₂-inch-thick pieces. Place, cut sides down, on the baking sheet. Bake for 15 to 20 minutes or until lightly toasted and crisp. Cool on a wire rack. Enjoy with an espresso and don't be afraid to dip!

LISABETH'S APRICOT BARS

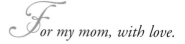 *For my mom, with love.*

CRUST

1 cup unsalted butter, softened
1²/₃ cups packed brown sugar
1²/₃ cups flour

TOPPING

¹/₃ cup melted butter
¹/₂ cup packed brown sugar
¹/₄ cup honey
¹/₄ cup apricot preserves
3 tablespoons heavy cream
2 cups sliced almonds
1 cup diced apricots or julienned
*   whole apricots (8 ounces)*

MAKES 36 BARS

CRUST: Cream the butter and brown sugar in a bowl. Add the flour and mix well. Spread over the bottom of a greased 9x13-inch baking pan. Bake at 350 degrees for 20 minutes; set aside.

TOPPING: Combine the melted butter, brown sugar, honey, apricot preserves and cream in a bowl. Add the almonds and apricots, stirring until thoroughly coated. Spread the almond mixture over the baked crust. Bake at 350 degrees for 20 to 25 minutes or until golden brown. Cool completely before cutting into bars.

SUE'S PULLED PORK BARBECUE SANDWICH

1 (3¹/2-pound) boneless pork loin
    roast (end of the loin), trimmed
    and cut into 1¹/2-inch cubes
1 large onion, finely chopped
1¹/2 tablespoons vegetable oil
¹/2 cup packed brown sugar
2¹/2 cups catsup
6 tablespoons cider vinegar
3 tablespoons Dijon mustard
1¹/2 tablespoons mustard seeds
1 tablespoon Worcestershire sauce
1 teaspoon soy sauce
1 teaspoon kosher salt
¹/2 teaspoon ground chipotle or
    cayenne
¹/2 teaspoon Tabasco sauce
8 sandwich rolls

COLESLAW

1¹/2 pounds cabbage, shredded
3 tablespoons Dijon mustard
1 tablespoon catsup
¹/2 tablespoon fennel seeds
2 small cloves of garlic, minced
¹/2 teaspoon celery seeds
¹/2 cup mayonnaise

SERVES 6 TO 8

PORK BARBECUE SANDWICH: Place the pork cubes in a large saucepan with water to cover. Bring to a boil; reduce the heat. Simmer slowly for about 1¹/2 hours or until the pork shreds easily with a fork. Skim off any foam from the surface of the water. Drain and shred the meat, discarding any fat; set aside. Sauté the onion in the oil in a large saucepan until tender. Add the brown sugar and stir until dissolved. Stir in the catsup, cider vinegar, Dijon mustard, mustard seeds, Worcestershire sauce, soy sauce, kosher salt, chipotle and Tabasco sauce. Bring to a boil; reduce the heat. Simmer, uncovered, for 30 minutes or until thick. Stir in the shredded pork. Simmer for 20 minutes. Divide the pork among the rolls and top each with coleslaw.

COLESLAW: Combine the cabbage, mustard, catsup, fennel seeds, garlic, celery seeds and mayonnaise in a bowl. Stir to mix well. Makes 1 quart.

PHIL'S STEAK SALAD WITH GRILLED VEGETABLES AND FETA CHEESE

This is a perfect salad to bring to a potluck or for a picnic. It is colorful and the flavors work well together.

A.R.R.

GRILLED VEGETABLE MARINADE

1/2 cup balsamic vinegar

3 tablespoons olive oil

1/2 teaspoon salt

1/2 teaspoon pepper

Assorted vegetables (bell peppers, red onion, squash)

BALSAMIC VINAIGRETTE

1/3 cup balsamic vinegar

1/4 cup honey

2 tablespoons red wine vinegar

2 tablespoons Dijon mustard

2 tablespoons chopped fresh basil and parsley

1 1/2 cups olive oil

STEAK SALAD

1 1/2 pounds sirloin steak

Salt and pepper to taste

3 cups Bibb lettuce or mixed greens

4 ounces crumbled feta cheese

SERVES 6 TO 8

GRILLED VEGETABLE MARINADE: Combine the balsamic vinegar, olive oil, salt and pepper in a bowl. Marinate the vegetables for 1 to 2 hours.

BALSAMIC VINAIGRETTE: Process the balsamic vinegar, honey, red wine vinegar, Dijon mustard, basil and parsley in a food processor or blender. Add the olive oil in a fine stream, processing until emulsified.

STEAK SALAD: Season the steak with salt and pepper. Grill until cooked to rare or desired doneness. Cool completely. Slice thinly; set aside. Grill the vegetables until tender. Toss the lettuce with the balsamic vinaigrette in a bowl. Arrange the dressed greens on a serving platter. Top with the steak slices, grilled vegetables and feta cheese.

KEVIN'S PORTOBELLO MUSHROOMS STUFFED WITH SUN-DRIED TOMATO AND ARUGULA PESTO

This recipe makes an impressive first course. The pesto is delicious in a pasta salad or, with heavy cream added to it, makes a wonderful sauce over pasta.

8 ounces dry-pack sun-dried
   tomatoes, rehydrated
3/4 pound fresh arugula (3/4 cup)
1 1/4 cups grated Romano cheese,
   divided
1/4 cup walnuts
3 tablespoons chopped garlic
12 tablespoons chopped fresh basil
   leaves
1 cup plus 2 tablespoons extra-
   virgin olive oil, divided
1 tablespoon balsamic vinegar
Salt and pepper to taste
12 portobello mushrooms, sliced
   horizontally in half
1 cup shredded sharp Cheddar
   cheese

SERVES 12

Place the sun-dried tomatoes, arugula, 1/2 cup Romano cheese, walnuts, garlic and basil in a food processor. With the machine running, drizzle in 1 cup olive oil to achieve a thick, pesto consistency. Combine 2 tablespoons olive oil, balsamic vinegar, salt and pepper in a bowl. Add the mushroom halves. Marinate at room temperature for at least 2 hours. Grill or broil the mushrooms for 1 to 2 minutes on each side; cool. Stir the remaining 3/4 cup Romano cheese and Cheddar cheese into the pesto. Spoon the pesto mixture over the bottom halves of the mushrooms. Cover with the mushroom tops. Place on a baking sheet. Bake at 350 degrees for 8 to 10 minutes or until heated through and the cheese is melted.

JIM'S STRAWBERRY-BLUEBERRY PIE

CRUST

1/3 cup cold water

1 teaspoon sugar

1/2 teaspoon salt

2/3 cup shortening

2 cups flour

FILLING

3 cups blueberries

2 cups strawberries, hulled and cut in half

3/4 cup sugar

1/3 cup cornstarch

ASSEMBLY

1 egg, beaten

1 1/2 teaspoons sugar

MAKES 1 (9-INCH) PIE

CRUST: Combine the water, sugar and salt in a bowl. Cut the shortening into the flour in a medium mixing bowl, using your fingertips to pinch the flour and shortening together and mixing until it resembles coarse meal. Add the water mixture slowly while tossing the flour mixture. Mix just until the dough comes together. Divide the dough in half and form into 2 flattened disks. Wrap in plastic wrap. Refrigerate for several hours or overnight. Remove from the refrigerator 1 hour before rolling out.

FILLING: Combine the blueberries, strawberries, sugar and cornstarch in a bowl.

ASSEMBLY: Roll out half the pastry dough on a lightly floured surface to a 12-inch circle. Fit into a 9-inch pie plate. Pour the berry filling into the crust. Roll out the remaining dough to a 12-inch circle. Place over the filling. Trim away any excess dough, leaving a 1/2-inch overhang. With your thumb and forefinger, roll the edge of the dough up and under the edge of the pie plate to form a border. Crimp to form a decorative crust. Brush the top crust with the beaten egg. Refrigerate the pie for 30 minutes to 1 hour or until the crust is well chilled. Just before baking, brush the pie with egg a second time and sprinkle with the sugar. Cut a few slits in the top crust with a sharp knife. Bake at 350 degrees in the lower third of the oven for 1 1/4 hours or until the crust is golden and the filling is bubbling.

KELLY'S GINGER PEAR CAKE

1/2 cup butter, softened
1/2 cup packed brown sugar
1/4 cup Vermont maple syrup or
    corn syrup
1/4 cup molasses
1 egg
1 1/2 cups flour
1 teaspoon baking soda
1/4 teaspoon salt
1/2 cup water
1 ripe pear, peeled and diced
1/4 cup crystallized ginger, minced
2 tablespoons grated lemon zest
2 tablespoons grated gingerroot
Confectioners' sugar or whipped
    cream
Pear slices and lemon zest curls for
    garnish

MAKES 1 (9-INCH) CAKE

Cream the butter and brown sugar in a bowl until light and fluffy. Beat in the maple syrup and molasses until creamy. Add the egg and mix well. Sift together the flour, baking soda and salt. Add the dry ingredients to the butter mixture alternately with the water, beginning and ending with the dry ingredients. Fold in the diced pear, crystallized ginger, lemon zest and gingerroot. Pour the batter into a greased and floured 9x9-inch baking pan. Bake at 350 degrees for about 30 minutes or until the cake starts to pull away from the sides of the pan. Let cool in the pan for 5 minutes. Invert onto a wire rack and cool. Serve dusted with confectioners' sugar or frosted with whipped cream. Garnish with pear slices and lemon zest curls.

MARY'S VEGETABLE TORTA WITH HERBED POLENTA CRUST

Mary Laulis, owner of The Bridge Street Bakery, a charming and lively spot for locals and visitors that is located next to the covered bridge, made this recipe for our friend Kitty Smyth's farewell memorial at the Round Barn Farm. We were fortunate enough to have Mary work for us at Cooking from the Heart before she created the bakery. Now she makes us beautiful wedding cakes and delicious breads that we serve at our weddings. Her bakery is our staff's favorite place to stop, sit, and relax with a cappuccino.

4 cups water

1 tablespoon chopped hot peppers

1 tablespoon chopped fresh basil leaves

1 tablespoon chopped fresh oregano leaves

1¹/3 cups cornmeal

1 teaspoon salt

¹/2 cup grated Parmesan cheese

1 onion, chopped

2 tablespoons chopped garlic

2 tablespoons butter or olive oil

1 carrot, chopped (1 cup)

1 red bell pepper, chopped (1 cup)

1 zucchini, chopped (2 cups)

2 cups fresh spinach leaves

1 pint ricotta cheese

6 eggs

1 teaspoon salt

¹/2 teaspoon pepper

2 tomatoes, sliced

1 cup shredded Cheddar cheese

SERVES 12 TO 15

Bring the water to a boil in a saucepan. Add the hot peppers, basil and oregano. Add the cornmeal, salt and Parmesan cheese slowly, whisking constantly. Stir for 3 to 5 minutes or until the mixture thickens. Pour into a 10-inch springform pan lined with parchment paper on the bottom or sprayed with vegetable spray. Chill for 10 minutes.

Sauté the onion and garlic in the butter in a skillet until tender. Add the carrot and red pepper and continue to cook. Stir in the zucchini and spinach. Cover and cook until the vegetables are tender. Whisk together the ricotta cheese and eggs in a bowl. Season with the salt and pepper. Fold in the cooked vegetables. Pour the ricotta mixture over the cornmeal mixture in the pan, spreading evenly. Top with the tomatoes and Cheddar cheese. Bake at 350 degrees for 50 minutes or until golden brown. Remove from the oven and cool slightly. Remove the side of the springform pan. Invert a plate over the torta and turn upside down. Remove the pan bottom and parchment paper. Invert the torta again onto a serving plate.

TIFFANY'S TUILE CIGARS WITH RASPBERRY CREAM

¹/₄ cup unsalted butter, softened

¹/₂ cup packed brown sugar

¹/₄ cup light corn syrup

¹/₂ cup flour

¹/₈ teaspoon cinnamon

Pinch of salt

³/₄ cup heavy cream

2 tablespoons raspberry jam

1 tablespoon confectioners' sugar

MAKES 18 COOKIES

Cream the butter and brown sugar in a bowl until mixed well. Beat in the corn syrup. Add the flour, cinnamon and salt; mix well. Refrigerate, covered, for 1 hour. Place the dough by 1-tablespoon portions on 2 greased cookie sheets. Smooth each piece of dough as thin as possible using a piece of plastic wrap. Bake for 10 to 11 minutes or until a dark caramel color and large bubbles form. Remove from the oven and cool for 30 seconds. (If any cookies have baked together at the edges, cut them apart with a sharp knife.) Roll each cookie gently around a wooden spoon handle to form a cigar shape, being careful because the mixture will be very hot. When cool, slide the cookies off the spoon handle. Work quickly or the cookies will harden. If they do, reheat in the oven until pliable.

Whip the cream until soft peaks form. Add the raspberry jam and confectioners' sugar. Whip just until stiff peaks form. Pipe the raspberry cream slowly into each end of the rolled cookies with a #5 straight pastry tip. Garnish with a dusting of confectioners' sugar.

NOTE: The dough may be stored in the refrigerator for up to 1 month.

VARIATION: Add finely chopped hazelnuts or pecans to the dough before baking. Flavor the dough with ¹/₈ teaspoon orange oil when mixing.

Index

For order information call
1-800-721-8029.